Tao of Healing

A Story of Georgia Integrative Medicine

Yoon Hang "John" Kim MD

D1125214

ISBN: 1496119401
ISBN 13: 9781496119407

CONTENTS

Preface   v

Part I: The Path   1

1   Finding the Flow   2
2   Investing in the Loss   16
3   Good Medicine   34
4   Mapping the Path   52

Part II: The People   69

Introducing the Team   70
5   Vena   72
6   Jeanne   81
7   Nola   96
8   Dorothy   105
9   Supporting Members   117

Part III: The Practice   123

10   Creating the Space   124
11   Tools for Healing   138
12   Good Business   154
13   A Day in the Life   169

Epilogue   181
Notes/Sources   185

PREFACE

In 2007, I found myself in Georgia, stranded without a job. It was an extremely difficult time. With limited financial resources and a family to support, I needed to find a source of income that would utilize my talents and experience. However, I wasn't simply in search of a job. I realized I had the opportunity to pursue something more lasting and meaningful.

This book tells the story of that journey, the confluence of events and good fortune which brought together a group of like-minded individuals and led to the creation of Georgia Integrative Medicine. It is a story of risk, reversals, and struggle. But far more importantly, it is also one of hope, strength, love, and compassion. It is told from my individual viewpoint, with additional insights from team members of the Georgia Integrative team.

In telling the story, I incorporate elements from Taoism, an ancient Chinese philosophy and religion famously articulated in the *Tao Te Ching*. These days, the word *Tao*, translated as "the way" or "path" has entered the mainstream, giving us books such as *The Tao of Pooh*, *The Tao of Poker*, and, yes, *The Tao of Dating*. These titles, while amusing, speak to a deeper truth: that the Tao is universal and all encompassing. I believe that the principles of the Tao can be a powerful force for individual and collective healing and transformation. It begins with the concepts of simplicity, balance, and power.

Our need for a new vision of medicine is beyond question. The state of health care in the United States is highly dysfunctional. We spend more money on health care than any country in the world, with dismal results. In 1997, the year I graduated from medical school, Americans spent $1.1 trillion on personal health care expenditures. By 2012, that figure had more than doubled to $2.8 trillion. At the same time, nearly 50 million Americans lack health insurance. Ongoing battles over reform reveal a deep divide in the way we perceive and approach health care. Despite our seeming obsession with health, diet, exercise, and nutrition, we continue to lag behind. A study released in 2013 examined causes of death in 17 of the world's most affluent nations and found the United States fared poorly, with some of the highest rates of heart disease, lung disease, obesity and diabetes in the developed world.

The Affordable Care Act, signed into law in 2010, has survived a challenge in the Supreme Court and is on schedule for full implementation by 2015. The legislation has been the subject of much controversy, debate, and criticism, but it is not clear that it will have much effect other than increasing access to the existing system, with its severe limitations. While seeking to remove the bureaucratic and structural obstacles that keep people from seeking and receiving treatment, the law does little to address the efficacy and quality of the health care available and does nothing to challenge the conventional form of medicine widely practiced in the U.S. This allopathic model, which focuses on treating the symptoms of illness rather than the root causes, is unsustainable.

My aim in writing this book is to help readers understand the complexity of the problem and to motivate them to harness their individual power to ignite a consciousness-raising revolution that promotes wellness across society. I hope our story will inspire others to begin similar communities with a shared mission, dedicated to the welfare and sustainability of each individual member.

PART I: THE PATH

道

George

thanks for having

tea with us.

John.

CHAPTER 1

FINDING THE FLOW

The tao that can be told is not the eternal Tao.
The name that can be named is not the eternal Name.
Tao Te Ching

So begins the *Tao Te Ching*, the foundational text of Taoism, an ancient Chinese philosophy and religion. While Tao literally translates as "the way," its meaning and significance are elusive. If it cannot be told and is unnamable, how are we to understand or recognize it? The *Tao Te Ching* is full of such enigmas and apparent paradoxes. *The master stays behind. That is why she is ahead. When nothing is done, nothing is left undone.* What are we to make of it?

The "way" referred to here is what the *Tao Te Ching* calls "the natural course" of one's life. It is the way of the universe. To be in sync with the Tao is to be in harmony with nature, with oneself, and with others. Following the Tao, there is peace, tranquility, and calm. There is a sense of rightness and purpose to daily life.

The 81 spare verses of the *Tao Te Ching* instruct us on how to act and behave in a manner that is harmonious with the Tao and with nature. Little is known about its author, Lao Tzu. He is believed to have lived during the sixth century B.C. He may have been a contemporary of Confucius and was possibly an archivist in one of China's many kingdoms. Even this limited information comes to us from unreliable sources and cannot be confirmed. Numerous translations of the *Tao Te Ching* exist and while they may vary in wording and syntax, the essential principles remain constant.

Anyone who has ever studied an Asian martial art will be familiar with elements of Taoism. In fact, the names of many martial arts refer directly to the Tao by ending in "do," the Japanese and Korean form of the Chinese word Tao. Thus we have judo (gentle way), aikido (way of harmonious energy) and tae kwon do (way of kicking and punching).

I first took tae kwon do in elementary school. Even at a young age, I found it fascinating that a smaller person could overcome a larger, seemingly stronger person by mastering the proper techniques and developing a resilient spirit. My first tae kwon do teacher, Master Bae, was well versed in several martial arts. His vast knowledge inspired me and I spent as much time as possible studying with him. As with most boys, I was more interested in the fighting aspect of tae kwon do, but Master Bae guided me toward learning about its spiritual qualities and the meaning of the Tao. For him, fighting represented a failure of conflict resolution. He believed that any true student of martial arts would naturally choose non-violence whenever possible. His reasoning was simple. Fighting is unpredictable and both parties risk injury. Non-violence assures the survival of both participants and resolves conflicts safely.

Master Bae often said that the study of martial arts should result in a situation in which one can run away from an assailant without fear. At first I found his teachings perplexing, but gradually I came to understand. Studying and applying martial arts has helped me to explore the least violent ways of conflict resolution and to develop my mind, body, and spirit. It also deepened my understanding of Taoism. While it can be practiced as a religion, I am more interested in Taoism's philosophical implications.

A key principle within Taoism, and perhaps the most difficult to explain, is that of *wu wei*, which translates as non-action or not doing. "Practice not doing," says the *Tao Te Ching*, "and everything will fall into place." This is commonly misinterpreted as an instruction to do nothing or to remain passive. In reality, it refers to the ability to act in a way that is so in sync with the natural way that it appears to be effortless. Think of a river flowing to the ocean. It follows a natural course. There is nothing forced about it, and yet there is movement.

I think of wu wei as spontaneous achievement. Many people find modern life a day-to-day struggle. They have not discovered the natural flow and as a consequence, suffer. Focused entirely on their own suffering and distracted by the challenges they face, they lack the heightened awareness or mindfulness that is necessary to wu wei. This stagnation is not a sign of weakness. It is a common fact of life. To return to our river metaphor, let's imagine the water has reached a large rock that prevents it from flowing on. As long as the water continues to beat against that rock, it will not pass. Mindfulness gives us insight into our own behavior. We can learn from our mistakes and avoid repeating them. Instead of fighting ourselves and those around us, we can act in accordance with our inner way of being and expend less energy in doing so. We too can go with the flow.

Recognizing and following one's inner way requires simplicity of thought and purpose. In Chinese, this simplicity is referred to as *pu*. It is believed to be the true nature of the mind unburdened by preconceived notions and beliefs. Free of learned labels, biases, and definitions, we become more flexible and able to perceive things as they really are. This condition is a natural consequence of wu wei.

While the attainment of simplicity (pu) and spontaneous action (wu wei) are individual benefits of being in sync with the Tao, there is a larger, more outward manifestation known as *te*. Translated most often as virtue, it also carries with it the connotation of a moral power that has the ability to influence others, thereby contributing to a more virtuous, ethical society.

From tae kwon do, I moved on to aikido. Eventually, on the recommendation of my aikido instructor, I took up tai chi. I began studying the short form Yang style of tai chi developed by Professor Cheng Man Ching. In addition to being a tai chi master, Professor Cheng received formal training in Chinese medicine and was an accomplished poet and painter. I was a fascinated to learn of a martial arts master who was also a physician. When I discovered that Professor Cheng passed away in 1975, I set about to find an instructor who had studied with him.

My initial search uncovered a teacher named Patricia living close by. This seemed too good to be true, so I continued to look. I finally settled on William Chen, a master who had studied under Professor Cheng and was highly regarded for his expertise. Unfortunately, he lived in New York, nowhere near me. By this time, I was out of medical school and had started my internship. Despite a lack of time and resources, I made regular trips to New York to learn from Master Chen. He found it curious that I managed to improve even though I only showed up once every few months. When I explained that I was using my vacation time to travel, he recommended a tai chi teacher he knew who lived in my area. Her name? Patricia.

The experience taught me a lesson. Had I gone with Patricia from the outset, it would have saved me considerable time and money, both of which were in short supply. However, my desire to find a "true master" blinded me to what was right in front of me all along. My journey took me far from home, but returned me to the place where I had started.

Tai chi teaches us to "invest in loss." In his writings, Professor Cheng explains that it is our first instinct to seek an immediate advantage over an opponent. Investing in loss, on the other hand, requires allowing our opponent to attack without offering any resistance. Instead, we draw our opponent's force away so that it becomes ineffective, and our counter even more powerful. Without knowing it, I had invested in loss by seeking out the best tai chi teacher. The fact that Master Chen explicitly recommended Patricia was a great honor. She proved to be an outstanding instructor and was responsible for locating my next teachers in California. Though I had come to her by a circuitous path, I believe that she gave me special attention because I had been Master Chen's pupil.

The Chinese tell the story of a man who found a horse. When his neighbors congratulated him on his good luck, he said, "We'll see." While riding the horse, the man's son fell off and was injured. Neighbors offered their sympathy. The man replied, "We'll see." Shortly thereafter, the country went to war and every able-bodied man was recruited into the army. The war was disastrous, with only one man in ten surviving. Because of his disability, the man's son was exempt from conscription. People agreed that in this world, fortune and misfortune are difficult to tell apart. Or, in the words of a fortune cookie I once opened, "What at first appears to be a calamity may give rise to good fortune."

The development of tai chi is attributed to a Taoist ascetic Zhang San Feng, who witnessed a snake defending itself from a bird of prey. Tai chi embodies the Taoist philosophy of yielding, relaxing and lessening of effort. It relies on relaxation, rather than muscular tension, in order to neutralize attacks. Some adherents refer to tai chi as a form of moving meditation because focusing the mind solely on the movements helps to bring about a state of mental calm and clarity. Yet the benefits of tai chi extend beyond those of traditional meditative techniques. Anyone can enter the temporary relaxed state of meditation. Tai chi is about being able to remain calm in the face of emotional or physical turmoil.

The study of tai chi integrates health, meditation, and martial arts. A few traditional schools cover all three aspects simultaneously while the majority of modern schools focus only on health. Tai chi training typically begins with a solo form, moving on to partner exercises known as "pushing hands," where each individual learns to sense a partner's balance. The next level of training may involve weapons such as a sword. The final phase can include free fighting and/or the cultivation of *qi*, the energy or life force that sustains the universe and all within it. Progressing through the stages of tai chi is a long-term proposition that requires dedication and focus. Even after studying and practicing tai chi for more than a decade, I feel that I have only just begun to understand its basic principles.

Once I had a taste of tai chi, I lost interest in all other martial arts. There is a depth to tai chi that I had not encountered in any other form. In Chinese, tai chi is called tai chi chuan, or, "supreme ultimate boxing." The supreme ultimate refers to the Taoist concept of duality, the complementary principles of yin and yang. Yin represents feminine, receptive, yielding energy while yang represents male, dominant, moving energy. These two forces are believed to reside in all aspects of life.

My personal view is that the highest level of tai chi is the application of its core tenets to non-violent conflict resolution. It is important to make the distinction between non-violence and weakness. To choose relaxation over tension, to act intently rather than forcefully, requires greater spiritual and emotional strength. It is much more challenging to overcome an opponent using a relaxed and intentional approach than it is to rely on brute force and aggression. This applies not only to physical confrontations, but also to challenges that arise in everyday life.

The Western phrase "when push comes to shove" refers to moments of extreme difficulty that reveal our true character, whether they involve health, family, finances, career, or any other aspect of our existence. When push comes to shove, how will we react? In times of adversity, tai chi can help us face and overcome obstacles with calmness and resolve.

Although there has been only limited research into the health benefits of tai chi, studies have shown its efficacy in lowering blood pressure, alleviating the effects of diseases such as osteoarthritis and fibromyalgia, and boosting cardiovascular health. This link between tai chi and improved health provides an insight into the kind of medicine I practice with my team at Georgia Integrative Medicine.

In its current form, the American system of health care is seriously flawed. A dysfunctional, bloated, fragmented behemoth, it is run by what I call the pharmaceutical-medical-insurance complex. Our health, our most basic need to survive, is inextricably linked to a system motivated not by our well-being, but by the almighty dollar. The truth is that the "health care" industry feeds on illness. Hospitals cannot survive without patients. A system that profits from disease cannot be truly interested in promoting health.

What we refer to as health insurance is really sickness insurance. We are conditioned to seek medical attention only when we are unwell. A growing number of people do not have primary care physicians with whom they meet on a regular basis, leaving them to browse through a provider directory when they need to visit a doctor. Sadly, when patients do make an appointment, the time spent in the waiting room can often exceed the time spent in consultation with the doctor.

In addition, the combined cost of insurance, medical visits, and prescriptions can make it prohibitive to visit a doctor. It is not uncommon even for those with insurance to weigh the benefits of make an appointment versus self-diagnosing and self-medicating. A friend who had just joined an HMO told me that the company had sent her a thick book in the mail. It was a guide to various illnesses, complete with symptoms and treatments. For each malady, she recalls, there was a list of things to try at home before visiting the doctor. She joked that the book had turned her into a hypochondriac. Every time she had a headache or a slight pain, she looked through the list of symptoms, convincing herself she had encephalitis or an aneurysm. At the same time, its function was to discourage her from seeing a doctor unless her symptoms became severe.

Health care in the United States has been commercialized to the point where it is difficult to distinguish from other retail services. Pharmaceutical companies spend more than $7.3 billion a year on advertising. Hospitals have competing billboards on the highway and glossy mass mailers. Urgent care centers entice new patients with offers of free gift cards for ice cream. Doctors admit to giving in to patients' requests for unnecessary tests because if they do not, the patients will move on to a competitor down the street who will meet their demands. Under pressure to see more and more patients, health professionals spend less and less time with each one, in most cases focusing only on the ailment that is causing immediate pain or discomfort.

This situation is not only dysfunctional. It is dangerous. Taking patient histories requires time and thoroughness. Ascertaining a patient's condition and all the different factors that may be contributing to the current problem necessitates an examination of the whole person, not merely the area that is exhibiting symptoms. There may be underlying causes or contributors that are not immediately apparent. In years past, it was the norm for people to have a general practitioner or family doctor who was familiar with their medical history. Nowadays, we have doctors diagnosing (or in some cases simply prescribing for) patients based on a few minutes' consultation after meeting them for the first time. Modern drugs have powerful side effects, and yet they are distributed without hesitation, in some cases inappropriately and with insufficient information. Some patients will mistakenly confuse a prescription with a cure. In other words, a drug that lowers blood pressure is not intended to give a patient free license to consume all the salt he wants.

The system is failing because it has placed the focus on disease, not on health. At Georgia Integrative Medicine, we are attempting something revolutionary. We practice a form of healing that integrates elements of traditional Western medicine with complementary and alternative medicine. But it does not stop there. We recognize that integrative medicine cannot be practiced effectively within a conventional environment. It must be housed in an integral organization, an organization that redefines the role of employer-employee and aims to create the highest good for both employees and patients.

In 1993, PBS aired a groundbreaking series, *Healing and the Mind*, hosted by veteran journalist Bill Moyers. Over five episodes, Moyers investigated the mind-body connection, interviewing physicians, patients, therapists and scientists across the country. He even traveled to China to explore the Chinese approach to medicine. Among those Moyers interviewed was Dr. David Eisenberg, the first U.S. medical exchange student sent to China by the National Academy of Sciences. When Moyers asked him about the difference between Chinese and Western medicine, Eisenberg noted that in Chinese culture, "how you live ultimately influences your health." Pointing out that the Chinese medical system is based on Taoism, he went on to say that "it's not just your physical well-being that determines your health, but also your behavior toward others."

We apply these principles on a daily basis at our clinic, not only in our interactions with patients, but with one another. Our methods are very different from those found in conventional workplaces. Remaining mindful of the Tao, we seek the path that keeps us in harmony physically, mentally, and socially. This necessitates real teamwork, joint decision making, and looking out for one another. Our approach puts spirituality at the center of healing and is reinforced by our motto: "Compassion, moderation and humility." I hope the community we have created at our clinic in Georgia will serve as a model for others.

Dr. Eisenberg told Bill Moyers that in Chinese tradition, "The doctor was part priest, part martial artist, part scholar and part empirical scientist. But most of all, he was a teacher.... The doctor tried to teach people the best way to live their lives." This notion of physician as teacher is not confined to Eastern medicine. The origin of the word "doctor" comes from the Latin word *docere*, meaning to teach. More than 2,000 years ago, Hippocrates, the father of Western medicine, said that there is a doctor within each one of us, referring to the natural healing force we all possess. Helping people recognize and draw on that force is part of my mission. Throughout my life, I have been fortunate to study and work with a number of highly skilled, knowledgeable, and wise mentors. It is my intent to pass on what I have learned to my patients and colleagues and in turn, continue to learn from them.

FINDING THE FLOW

To understand what we are doing at our clinic and how and why we do it, it is helpful to return to the beginning of my own personal journey into medicine. A brief review of the history of modern medicine and an explanation of integrative medicine are also useful. One of the fallacies surrounding non-Western medicine is that it is unscientific. As someone who has always had a deep interest in and respect for science (my undergraduate major was chemistry), I have no time for those who purport to be miracle workers or make outlandish claims. As a physician, I am interested in therapies that are safe, proven, and effective.

Chapter 2

INVESTING IN THE LOSS

Knowing ignorance is strength.
Tao Te Ching

Someone recently asked me if I always wanted to be a doctor, and the answer is, not consciously. My wife Vena, whom I have known since high school, tells me that even then, I exhibited an ability to help and heal people. Vena says that if she complained of her arm hurting, invariably I would know where to apply pressure to ease the pain. My parents would make similar comments about my propensity for healing. I talked about acupuncture points and pressure points the way some teenagers talked about sports or music. I do know that I loved science, and chemistry was a natural choice for me when I landed at Beloit College as an undergraduate.

At Beloit, we were encouraged to express intellectual curiosity and to "reinvent" ourselves through exploration and self-discovery. The faculty was immensely helpful and supportive. Professors went the extra mile to ensure that everyone had an opportunity to develop professional interests through experiential learning.

I found two fields of chemistry most appealing. The first field was physical chemistry, which deals with the interactions and transformations of materials as governed by the laws of thermodynamics and kinetics. Thermodynamics refers to the transfer of energy from one form or location to another. Kinetics refers to how quickly the reaction will take place. An appropriate analogy is to think of a car. Thermodynamics asks the question, "What is the likelihood of this car starting?" Kinetics asks, "How fast can the car go?"

Energetics is defined as the energy relations and transformations of a physical, biological, or chemical system. The advantage of learning physical chemistry was that it gave me an understanding of the energetics of chemical reactions. This became invaluable to me later when I began to study the energy healing techniques that have become an important component of my medical practice.

The second field of interest was biochemistry. Biochemistry is the chemistry of life and living things. Two biochemical processes, photosynthesis and the citric acid cycle, are central to life. Photosynthesis is the conversion of light energy into chemical energy by living organisms. The raw materials are carbon dioxide and water, the energy source is sunlight, and the end products are oxygen and energy-rich carbohydrates. This process is the most important of all biochemical reactions, since nearly all life depends on it. It is a complex process occurring in higher plants, phytoplankton, algae, as well as bacteria such as cyanobacteria. By contrast, the citric acid cycle is how we convert carbohydrates, with the help of oxygen, into carbon dioxide and water to generate a form of usable energy.

My study of biochemistry helped me to understand how photosynthesis and the citric acid cycle form a balance in the energy equation of life. Plants use light energy to convert carbon dioxide and water into energy-rich carbohydrates. Animals use the products of photosynthesis—carbohydrates and oxygen—to create vital forms of energy in the body while releasing carbon dioxide and water.

The study of biochemistry also revealed how nutrition provides biochemical pathways with raw materials and how nutrition can influence the biochemical pathways. For example, if you eat foods that cause inflammation in the body, the natural consequence is inflammation of biochemical pathways. The natural consequence of high inflammation is an accelerated course of illness. Over the last 150 years, the United States dramatically increased agricultural production by implementing industrial production methods and management techniques. The result was mass production of crops, factory farms, and cheaper food. Items that were once considered a luxury, such as meat, became widely available. However, these innovations came at a cost, one of which is the proliferation of foods that are more likely to produce inflammation. Naturally, illness followed.

Biochemistry, I saw, was a manifestation of the Tao in living things. In Taoist philosophy, plants are categorized as yin and animals as yang. Yin energy is receptive, dormant, and supports yang energy. Yang energy is active, dominant, and draws upon the yin energy. Photosynthesis, the process by which yin energy is created, provides support to yang energy. Oxygen and carbohydrates, a byproduct of photosynthesis, unlock usable energy for animals, ensuring their survival. To me, this symbiosis illustrates the ageless principles of the Tao that continue on in the modern world.

Although I love science, I don't like research, and this limited my career options. Engineering was a possibility, as was sales, but I decided on medical school. I was in for a rude awakening. "Suffering" is the word that best describes the first two years, during which time we crammed in all our basic science courses. People often talk about how the Asian educational system relies on rote memorization, but there are disciplines in Western medicine that are just as mechanical. Coming from an undergraduate environment that valued intellectual curiosity, I found myself ill prepared for medical school. Most of my time was spent memorizing vast amounts of information in order to pass tests. There was no guidance on how to become a healer. I soon realized that medical school was about persistence, not smartness.

While the first two years of medical school were a blur of frustration and difficulty, the last two years were vastly more enjoyable. The second half of my training took place in clinical settings. Although the experience was intense, I thrived in the clinic. As medical students, we were fortunate to participate in a mentoring style of experiential learning where we learn from experienced personnel in the field. Often, we learned from the nurses, other medical students and residents, and most importantly, from our patients.

This period also marked a milestone in my personal life. My longtime friend from high school, Vena, had gone off to college in California. During my first semester of college, I became homesick and wrote to all my friends. Vena wrote back. We began corresponding and ended up writing each other every day. We were married while I was in medical school.

At the time, my interests in alternative healing modalities were met with advice to keep my interests in the art of medicine to myself and to explore further the science of medicine through research. I listened to that advice and found teachers who helped guide me and keep me centered in the Tao.

Art was a biochemistry professor at medical school. A patient, intelligent, and compassionate individual, he was successful personally and professionally. Art taught me about the importance of servant leadership.

I learned about serving the needs of people and inspiring them to discover their passion through work. Art excelled at helping people find ways to incorporate the things they loved into their lives. For instance, one graduate student's life appeared to revolve around socializing rather than research. His interests included fine wine and beer. Art patiently guided the student to complete his studies and steered him to a career involving the biochemistry of microbrewing.

Most medical students study biochemistry by memorizing pathways. I learned biochemistry by designing and conducting research experiments. This experience helped me to develop a hands-on feel for biochemistry rather than adopting the rote memorization approach used by my peers. The understanding of biochemistry would become a cornerstone of my practice at Georgia Integrative Medicine. By grasping the relationship between yin and yang and its application in the biochemistry of our bodies, we can use nutrition to influence the biochemical pathway and achieve optimal results.

My passion for biochemistry led me to invest two extra years in medical school performing research projects. As a result of my interest and work, I won the Howard Hughes Fellowship, a prestigious award given to promising scientists. During the fellowship, I focused my research on pharmacology, the science of how medications influence our biochemistry. Looking back, pharmacology was a natural fit for me because of its integration of chemistry, biochemistry, and medicine. Pharmacology also gave me a strong basis for understanding how supplements, vitamins, and herbs can help with the healing process. More importantly, it gave me an understanding of how we can better harness the power of medications.

When it came time to take up a residency, I chose family medicine because it offered general training. I knew that my training of choice, integrative medicine, did not exist. I chose to pursue training as a primary care physician so I would be capable of providing care in a number of settings such as hospitals, emergency rooms, and clinics.

While I found my training in family medicine immensely valuable, the tide of medicine was turning away from the provision of care to the business of medicine. Patient visits became transactions. Everyone became visibly stressed, especially the office staff who had to deal with volumes of insurance paperwork. The profession of medicine was caving to the pressures of the profit motive.

The inconsistencies were obvious. For instance, if physicians believed in promoting wellness, their lifestyles did not reflect it. I was consistently averaging more than 80 hours a week trying to do everything the system required me to do. Working in a high-pressure environment took its toll on me in every aspect of my life.

In August 1999, as I advanced to the last year of my residency in family medicine, I felt conflicted about the progress of my medical career. I had a vision of how I wanted to practice medicine, and I was frustrated in my endeavors to align myself with that vision. Every day felt like a struggle. Completing the residency in family medicine would lead to a relatively well-paying job, but at a high cost to me and to my family. My sense was that the economic pressures on physicians would continue to worsen. I could see that if I continued, I would end up, like many people, compromising my ideals and taking the path of least resistance.

The *Tao Te Ching* asks, "Do you have the patience to wait till your mud settles and the water is clear? Can you remain unmoving till the right action arises by itself?" Accordingly, I took three months off to reflect on my course of action. I spent one month in the Chequamegon-Nicolet National Forest in the Northwoods of Wisconsin. I meditated, practiced tai chi, and fasted. During one meditation session, I experienced an intense spiritual awakening. I felt the enormously comforting sensation of being connected with the universe. A brief, but powerful message came to me: "preventive medicine."

Until that time, I was not aware of the field of preventive medicine. I ended my meditation and fasting and went to the library to research it. I discovered that preventive medicine is a specialty recognized by the American

Board of Medical Specialties. To my surprise, there was a residency in preventive medicine run by the University of California, San Diego (UCSD) and San Diego State University (SDSU). I felt particularly drawn to the program in San Diego. Months before, I had visited the city for a conference and fallen in love with it. Walking on a beach at sunset, I had prayed for an opportunity to live and work in San Diego.

It turned out that one of the interviewers for the San Diego program was a physician who had previously trained with me. My research interests, especially the Howard Hughes Fellowship, tipped the scales in my favor, and I was offered an early acceptance position.

At the same time, I was accepted to the Medical Acupuncture for Physicians course at the University of California, Los Angeles. While waiting for the preventive medicine residency to start the following year, I immersed myself in the study of Chinese language, Chinese medicine, tai chi, qi gong, and meditation.

This was also a time for growth in my personal relationship. Vena was in the process of completing her master's degree in accounting. I took a job as an insurance medical examiner to help pay the bills, and Vena took a temporary position. We spent a lot of time together. Looking back, I feel fortunate to have had a space and time when I was able to invest in developing and reinventing myself, but most of all to reconnect with Vena.

Our relationship had suffered from the busy years I spent in medical school and as a resident. This respite from training gave us an opportunity to rediscover one another.

When the preventive residency began, I found it reminiscent of my undergraduate experience, which had valued intellectual curiosity and discovery. We were given clear goals, objectives, and guidance. As an added bonus, the residency paid for me to obtain a master's degree in public health from San Diego State. As part of the residency, I worked with a number of different institutions, including Balboa Naval Hospital, Kaiser Permanente, and San Diego County, in addition to SDSU and UCSD. Perhaps the most important lesson I learned was that there are no two preventive medicine physicians doing the same work. In the world of preventive medicine, one has to invent one's own career. It is not for everyone, but I loved every minute of it.

It was a very busy two years, but it felt effortless, unlike my time in family medicine. I did not experience the same stress because I was being positively stimulated. My life was flowing in a natural way, the result of being one with the Tao. I felt at home in preventive medicine. I had found my Tao of medicine. I created acupuncture programs at two community institutions. I learned how to design and conduct clinical trials involving human participants. I also honed my medical scholarship skills as I worked on my thesis. The training was extremely useful and provided a strong foundation for the work I do today.

During a seminar at UCSD I met Dr. Vincent Fellitti, who directed Kaiser Permanente's Positive Choice Wellness Center in San Diego. The center is a state-of-the-art institution dedicated to helping people achieve weight loss through a variety of programs, including medical weight management, nutrition counseling, fitness testing and instruction, personal training, exercise classes, and biofeedback. I consider Vincent a visionary who correctly predicted the obesity epidemic.

While I disagree with the extreme approach to weight loss focused on very low calorie intake, I was impressed with the integration of psychological growth programs, counseling, physical activity, and nutrition classes. Vincent recommended I initiate a small pilot program involving a group of the center's most difficult patients, those who had experienced multiple failures while trying to lose weight. My methods were severely limited as I was restricted to using only group therapy and no other healing modalities.

I was dealing with professional patients who were highly skilled and vested in defeating program protocols. In other words, they were veterans and knew how to manipulate the system. I knew that the medical approach would be unsuccessful, but I also knew I would learn a lot from these patients. I drew on all my past training to meet the challenge. In the end, it was my martial arts training that proved the most useful in providing a solution.

Zen meditation emphasizes the development of mindfulness, which can best be described as a state of attentive awareness of oneself and one's environment. My tae kwon do teacher, Master Bae, taught me that mindfulness is a form of mental technology that is applicable in almost all situations. In the martial art of aikido, *randori* refers to a form of practice in which multiple attackers simultaneously converge on a defender. The secret of defending against them is relaxation and mindful application of evasion and neutralization tactics on the nearest attacker, followed by throwing that attacker into the next attacker, and so on.

I began by changing the name of the group, which had been given the unfortunate moniker "Losers." I called them the "Survivors." I then shifted the focus from weight loss to wellness. Instead of weighing in at every meeting, the usual practice for weight loss programs, participants were weighed once a month. The purpose was to have them evaluate their overall wellness rather than fixate on how much weight they had lost or gained.

This approach is in the tradition of a Zen koan, a riddle-like question that should be answered not on an intellectual, but an intuitive level. Perhaps the most well-known Zen koan asks, "What is the sound of one hand clapping?"

I wanted the "Survivors" to ask themselves, "Where is my wellness?"

Each participant was paired with a wellness buddy to provide mutual support. They were encouraged to check with each other on a daily basis. Twice a week, we met to discuss wellness strategies. I insisted that each person pay a nominal fee, intended to demonstrate his or her commitment to the program and its goals. As I had anticipated, in the third week, one of the participants exploded. Frustrated and angry, he complained that I was not helping him to lose weight. Although his outrage was directed at me, there was no need for me to try and defend my methods. The group's members responded strongly, reminding him that they were supposed to be letting go of the obsession about weight loss and focusing instead on promoting their own wellness. At that moment, I recognized that even though I was the physician in the room, they were the experts. Their addiction to food had overcome all medical and surgical protocols for weight loss. If that same resilience could be put toward cultivating wellness, imagine the possibilities.

The pilot program eventually came to an end. I believe that it represented a threat to the mainstream medical system because there was no product to sell, no supplements, no powders or pills or medication. The idea that a purely mental approach could work where material technologies had failed contravenes conventional wisdom. When the program was over, I was offered a job where I was able to customize individual wellness programs for patients. I loved it.

As a staff physician at Kaiser Permanente, I made a good living. Vena and I were very happy living in San Diego. By this time, our son had been born. With family living close by and everything we needed within a 20-minute drive, we enjoyed a comfortable lifestyle. It would have been easy enough to stay on that course indefinitely. Yet despite all outward signs, I was experiencing a sense of disharmony, a disruption to the natural flow. Kaiser Permanente is a not-for-profit organization, but it is also a huge bureaucracy, with more than 3.5 million members in Southern California alone. Although my work was rewarding, I still felt constrained by the conservatism of the medical establishment and its artificial rules and regulations.

After meditating at length and considering my options, I decided to uproot my family and leave San Diego for what I believed was an unparalleled opportunity. I was one of four physicians selected to participate in the Program in Integrative Medicine at the University of Arizona in Tucson. The program is the brainchild of Dr. Andrew Weil, whom *The New York Times* said has "arguably become America's best-known doctor." Dr. Weil founded the Arizona Center for Integrative Medicine, based at the university. In addition to serving as professor of medicine and public health, Dr. Weil is the author of several best-selling books. He is widely regarded as an expert on alternative medicine, medicinal plants, and nutrition.

Integrative medicine, as defined by Dr. Weil's center, refers to "healing-oriented medicine that takes account of the whole person, including all aspects of lifestyle. It emphasizes the therapeutic relationship between practitioner and patient, is informed by evidence, and makes use of all appropriate therapies." Integrative medicine uses a mindful approach to medicine by balancing healing and curing, Eastern and Western practices, and conventional and alternative medicine.

At the outset of the fellowship, we were introduced to the work of cultural anthropologist Angeles Arrien, author of *The Four-Fold Way: Walking the Paths of the Warrior, Teacher, Healer and Visionary*. The four principles outlined in her book were presented as models for how we should approach the fellowship and one another. They are:

1. The Way of the Warrior: Show up, and choose to be present.
2. The Way of the Healer: Pay attention to what has heart and meaning.
3. The Way of the Visionary: Tell the truth without blame or judgment.
4. The Way of the Teacher: Be open to outcome, not attached to outcome.

Investing in the Loss

At the time, I had no idea of the deep impact these simple statements would have on my life. Learning to integrate these principles harmoniously was one of the most difficult and crucial lessons of the entire fellowship.

When I was in attendance, the integrative medicine program was two years long. Since then, it has been shortened considerably and supplemented with online learning. While online instruction is convenient and no doubt provides a wonderful opportunity to novice physicians interested in integrative medicine, I feel fortunate that I was able to interact directly with so many masters in the field for a full two years. The advantages of participating in the residential fellowship were tremendous. The experience was beneficial on so many levels. I learned to fine tune mind-body medicine, energy medicine, acupuncture, nutrition, supplements, and herbal medicine. I met many wonderful people who became friends and taught me a great deal.

Not least of these was Dr. Weil himself. He proved to be a sincere person who embodied the three treasures of the Tao: compassion, moderation, and humility. I was especially impressed with his down-to-earth demeanor and his modesty. He was always willing to learn from others. We hiked together, cooked, and engaged in lively, thought-provoking discussions. Until I met him, I did not understand the power of a community with a shared vision. Of all the lessons he taught me, this was perhaps the most important.

I had gone to Arizona with the goal of gaining further knowledge, but it was not exactly as I had expected. At first I spent most of my time reading and researching, but the truth was that my clinical and medical education was already quite far advanced by then. A faculty member remarked to me, "You came here to seek a master, but you're already a master, and you have to be your own apprentice." This observation affected me profoundly. After that, I began focusing on my inner development, hiking and meditating in search of my true self.

Seeing how Dr. Weil had built his own supportive community made me realize that I needed to find a way to create my own community of like-minded individuals. Dr. Weil was fond of saying that the first step of a revolution is to create a counterculture. My difficulties had always been related to my desire to go against prevailing norms, against "the establishment." The answer then, might lie in creating an alternative model with its own set of values. Integrative medicine, which offers a new way of approaching health, is the ideal field for innovation.

During my two-year fellowship in Arizona, I had the opportunity to visit a number of prominent integrative medicine programs across the country. I spent a few days at each facility, observing their business models, strategic planning and operations. After visiting and studying a number of these programs, I began to see a recurring theme. All of them were losing money. The people who ran them suffered under the misconception that just because they were promoting a virtuous form of medicine, the funding would come. I had a different view. It was clear to me that in order for integrative medicine to survive, it would require a balance of good medicine and good business practices.

Chapter 3

GOOD MEDICINE

Ignoring knowledge is sickness.
Tao Te Ching

Until the late 19th century, it was widely believed that living organisms arose spontaneously from nonliving matter, a process referred to as spontaneous generation. According to this theory, mice could appear suddenly in grain and maggots would infiltrate spoiled meat, seemingly from nowhere. The origin of this idea can be traced to the Greek philosopher Aristotle, who stated that it is readily observable that the dew on plants creates aphids, fleas rise from putrid matter, and alligators come from decaying logs. The pioneering scientists who disproved spontaneous generation and other long-held misconceptions helped to bring medicine into the modern age.

French chemist and microbiologist Louis Pasteur is best known to us for pasteurization, the process by which we stop milk from souring. Pasteur is considered one of the founders of microbiology and was one of the first scientists to show that microorganisms cause disease, leading to his creation of vaccines for diseases such as rabies. In a famous experiment, he set out to prove that the fermentation process is caused by the growth of microorganisms, and that the growth of microorganisms is not due to spontaneous generation. Pasteur boiled beef broth in specially designed flasks with long, swanlike necks designed to keep dust particles out. When the flask was kept intact, and no air was allowed to enter, the broth remained sterile. However, when Pasteur broke the neck of the flask and exposed the fluid to the outside air, the broth became cloudy and contaminated. This experiment provided some of the most compelling evidence against the theory of spontaneous generation.

Pasteur's contemporary, German physician Robert Koch, had an interest in anthrax, a deadly disease that was then prevalent among livestock. Hoping to prove that bacteria caused the disease, Koch inoculated mice using slivers of wood containing anthrax bacilli taken from the spleens of farm animals that had died of the disease. He inoculated another group of mice with blood taken from healthy animals. The first group died of the illness while the second group remained healthy. This confirmed that disease could be transmitted via the blood of sick animals. Using pure cultures of anthrax bacilli, Koch went on to demonstrate that even bacilli that had never been in contact with any animal could also cause the disease. He went on to continue his work in bacteriology and received the 1905 Nobel

Prize in medicine or physiology for investigations and discoveries related to tuberculosis.

The work of these innovative scientists led to greater understanding of the causes and transmission of disease, paving the way for the implementation of new medical technology such as immunizations, antibiotics, and antiseptic techniques. The huge strides made at the turn of the 20th century profoundly impacted the health of populations who had access to these new resources, contributing to an increase in life expectancy of more than 30 years over the next century. The control of infectious diseases through improved sanitation, access to clean water, and healthier food sources was a major breakthrough in public health with widespread benefits.

As the rate of infectious diseases declined, patterns of illness shifted. With significant advances in public health knowledge and activity, dreaded diseases such as tuberculosis, cholera and pneumonia were no longer the leading causes of death. Replacing them were the chronic diseases with which we have become so familiar. A 2011 report from the National Institute on Aging and World Health Organization noted that, "Over the next 10 to 15 years, people in every world region will suffer more death and disability from such noncommunicable diseases as heart disease, cancer, and diabetes than from infectious and parasitic diseases."

Lifestyle-related risk factors play a greater role than ever in the proliferation of these chronic diseases. The factors include tobacco use, physical inactivity, poor nutrition and diet, alcohol consumption, and risky sexual behaviors. The much-discussed obesity epidemic can be linked directly to two of these factors: physical inactivity and poor nutrition.

This seismic shift presents an enormous challenge to the health care system. When infectious diseases were pervasive, scientific discoveries led to greater comprehension of the causes of illness and the development of appropriate treatments and procedures to fight them: antibiotics, vaccines, and sterilization. As long as the cause of an illness could be isolated to a pathogen, a vaccine could be effective in preventing it and antibiotics in treating it. We fought and largely overcame infectious diseases through a comprehensive approach involving medical treatment (antibiotics), preventive medicine (vaccinations), and public health initiatives (sanitation, cleaner water, and safer food).

Chronic diseases are much more complex. Our current medical model has failed to contain conditions such as obesity, diabetes, and heart disease. There are three main reasons for this failure.

The first is that our strategies for treating chronic conditions are heavily influenced by our experience of treating infectious diseases. Take a disease such as tuberculosis. It is primarily an airborne disease, which means it can be transmitted via a sneeze or a cough, nearly instantaneously. By contrast, chronic conditions emerge over a long period of time, making it difficult to pinpoint and study the definitive cause of the illness. There are often multiple contributing factors, including environment, genetics, nutrition, and other behavioral determinants. Despite the fact that we have an arsenal of medications and medical procedures to "successfully" treat chronic diseases, they continue to wreak havoc on our society.

The second reason is that the infectious disease model of medicine allowed the patient to play a passive role. Most antibiotics are prescribed for days or weeks while the individual is feeling sick and is highly motivated to take the medication. Most medications for chronic illness consist of a lifetime regimen of taking medicine for conditions with no appreciable symptoms. The optimal management, treatment, and prevention of chronic diseases require a comprehensive approach that encompasses behavioral changes in the form of lifestyle adjustments: good nutrition, increased physical activity, and stress management.

Imagine an individual who has to take medication over one week when he or she is feeling miserable. That person is highly likely to complete the course of prescribed antibiotics. Now imagine another individual who feels "well." That person is asked to make substantial lifestyle changes that may at first seem inconvenient, difficult, or unpleasant. It's easy to see how motivation and compliance favor the infectious disease model over the program of comprehensive lifestyle changes.

As a result, most health care systems lack effective, integrated health education and promotion strategies. Instead of having a systemic approach to implementing wellness, the responsibility to maintain wellness is passed off first to physicians and then to patients, without any meaningful guidance. It is a system in which the blind appear to be leading the blind.

This is the third reason our current model is failing. Previously, society recognized the importance of controlling infectious disease and saw the need for campaigns, regulations, and programs in support of public health. Today, there are very few American cities where people can combine walking and the use of public transportation. Many of the newer housing developments do not even have sidewalks. Fast food businesses are slow to adopt simple strategies that would make their food healthier. Foods lack nutritional value due to our farming practices. Even something that should be healthy, such as fish, contains contaminants.

Food is perhaps the area of greatest confusion for the general public. Food that is marketed as "healthy" often isn't. People follow food fads without any real understanding of what they are doing and what the health implications might be. I once attended a break-fast meeting and saw a man perusing the buffet table. He explained that he was on a "no carb" diet and was looking for something he could eat. He finally settled on cream cheese. At first I thought he was joking, but then I watched as he loaded up his plate with a heaping serving of cream cheese and proceeded to eat that and nothing else. We are bombarded with so many mixed messages about what is and isn't good for us. The modern lifestyle, with its hectic pace, is not conducive to healthy eating.

Fewer people cook with fresh ingredients. Processed and junk foods are cheap and readily available. In some areas, healthy food is difficult to locate. The phrase "food desert" is now used to describe areas in which there is no access to healthy foods such as fruits, vegetables, whole grains, and other items considered necessary for a balanced diet. These neighborhoods lack supermarkets and grocery stores and many residents do not have cars, making it difficult to reach healthy food retailers that are not in the immediate area.

The consequences of our failure are clear. According to the Centers for Disease Control:

- More than one-third of U.S. adults are obese
- 25.8 million Americans suffer from diabetes
- 79 million people over the age of 20 are considered "prediabetic"

- One in four deaths is caused by heart disease
- 1 in 3 U.S. adults suffers from high blood pressure

In another departure from the infectious disease model, the most common chronic diseases are linked. In other words, if you are obese, you are at higher risk for diabetes and heart disease. If you have high blood pressure, you are more likely to develop heart disease or have a stroke.

The transition from infectious to chronic or noncommunicable diseases requires a corresponding shift in the way we think about our health. As long ago as 1941, medical historian Henry E. Sigerist noted that, "Health...is not simply the absence of disease; it is something positive, a joyful attitude towards life, and a cheerful acceptance of the responsibilities that life puts upon the individual." This is my favorite definition of health. It describes a state of well-being that encompasses social, professional, physical, recreational, emotional, and biological dimensions. It is an early reflection of society's changing consciousness regarding what it means to be truly well. Wellness is not simply the lack of illness.

This holistic view of health takes into account the entire person rather than focusing on individual physiological functions or organs. It considers factors such as biology, biochemistry, anatomy, social network, profession, family life, personal history and more. Holistic medicine recognizes that the emotional, mental, spiritual, and physical elements associated with each person comprise a system, and attempts to treat the whole person within that context, concentrating on the causes of illness as well as the symptoms. This is in opposition to the generic approach to medicine in which doctors treat symptoms rather than individuals. Holistic medicine highlights each person's individuality and can tailor treatments accordingly. It also places an emphasis on the patient's responsibility for his or her own wellness.

Dr. Bernie Siegel, a Yale University surgeon, was an early advocate of holistic medicine. He was also one of my teachers in medical school. Dr. Siegel believes that while the biology of disease is responsible for pathology, the biology of the individual is responsible for healing. Over the course of his career, he treated numerous cancer patients and noticed an interesting phenomenon. Some individuals appeared to heal much more easily than others, in a process known as "spontaneous remission." Dr. Siegel decided to take a closer look and interviewed patients who demonstrated remarkable recoveries. In 1978, he formed Exceptional Cancer Patients (ECaP), a group of people dedicated to using inner healing resources to deal with the challenges of cancer and other serious illnesses. Dr. Siegel holds that:

- Healing can take place even when there is no cure.
- Unconditional love heals.
- Patient empowerment is a key factor in healing.

- The conscious and unconscious powers of the mind should be mobilized against disease
- Art is a therapeutic way to express your emotions.

Dr. Siegel's wife Bobbie coined the term "clergery" to refer to his work, whereby he could "combine the support and guidance of a minister with the resources and expertise of a physician." I met many of Dr. Siegel's extraordinary patients in his workshops. When my own mother was diagnosed with breast cancer, I reached out to him for help. We followed his advice and I am grateful to report that she is now a two-time breast cancer survivor. Dr. Siegel's principles have deeply influenced the way I view medicine. He was also the one who recommended I train with Dr. Weil in Arizona, an experience that proved to be transformative.

Dr. Siegel's colleagues in the larger medical community have generally not been receptive to holistic medicine and it operated outside the mainstream for a long time. Many medical professionals considered holistic practitioners heretics who rejected the scientific method. As a result, while introducing important ideas regarding the integration of mind, body, and spirit, holistic medicine has not been able to make significant inroads into conventional medicine. What saved it from extinction was the response of the public. Today, holistic medicine is frequently associated with the practice of alternative medicine. However, while the practices of holistic medicine may not be widely accepted within mainstream medicine, the concept of a mind-body connection has gained traction and is increasingly acknowledged as an important factor in patient care.

The terms "alternative medicine" and "complementary medicine" are often used interchangeably, but they are not the same thing. There are important differences. Alternative medicine refers to the use of a non-mainstream approach as a substitute for a conventional medicine. In general, alternative therapies are closer to nature, cheaper, and less invasive than conventional therapies. Some alternative treatments are scientifically validated; others are not. It could be something as simple as taking herbal supplements rather than pharmaceuticals for a minor medical condition.

Complementary medicine combines alternative and conventional medical approaches. An example would be a cancer patient suffering from nausea who uses acupressure or acupuncture to reduce the side effects of conventional treatment. In this example, complementary medicine plays a supporting role to conventional medicine.

Complementary medicine can be very effective if practiced properly. However, there are also situations in which a complementary approach can have tragic outcomes. St. John's Wort is a well-known herb used throughout the ages to treat a number of conditions, including anxiety, depression, and sleep disorders. If a transplant patient uses St. John's Wort, however, it can interfere with the immunosuppressant medication used to prevent organ rejection, creating a very dangerous situation. This is only one of a number of medications known to interact negatively with this particular herb. Knowing which combinations are harmless and which can be potentially fatal is crucial to the safe practice of complementary medicine.

Likewise, there are risks associated with alternative medicine. I have patients who use oil of oregano to treat occasional sinusitis. Oil of oregano can be an effective alternative to antibiotics when sinusitis is in its early stages, without fever, chills and other constitutional symptoms. However, it is not appropriate to use oil of oregano when a patient is suffering from a more serious form of sinusitis complicated by respiratory symptoms.

The misuse of alternative medicine can have devastating consequences, especially in cases of life-threatening illnesses such as cancer. Rejecting a treatment that has an established track record in favor of an unproven therapy with unknown safety implications can be disastrous. A physician colleague of mine had a form of cancer that is known to respond well to chemotherapy. He asked for my advice in seeking an alternative treatment. I advised him that we should be guided by mindfulness to pursue the most effective form of treatment rather than allow ourselves to be guided by fear, bias or prejudice.

Another problem with using alternative medicine is the possibility of delaying or missing a diagnosis. Many medical problems are much easier to treat if detected early. Initiating a healing modality without the benefit of correct diagnosis is like trying to navigate without a compass. In the case of a disease such as cancer, a delayed or missed diagnosis can be fatal.

Conventional medicine is the term we use to refer to the pharmaceutical and surgical approach most U.S. doctors employ. It is the kind of medicine most Americans encounter in clinics and hospitals. While often expensive and invasive, it is still the best and most obvious choice for certain situations, such as a traumatic injury or a life-threatening stroke. Dr. Weil himself said, "If I were hit by a bus, I'd want to be taken immediately to a high-tech emergency room." Similarly, as a doctor, if my goal is for the patient to get better, I would be foolish to reject any system of medicine that has demonstrated efficacy, be it Western or Eastern. I want to have all possible tools at my disposal and choose those which best serve the circumstances. The analogy is this: if really bad people are trying to break into your house, it's no time to be a pacifist. Similarly, if you are fighting for your life, you don't want to fight with one hand tied behind your back.

Good Medicine

For generations, conventional medicine was the only choice for most Americans. In recent years, however, more and more people have turned to alternative and complementary medicine as they become disillusioned with mainstream medicine. Part of this frustration comes from the increasingly impersonal nature of corporate medicine. As health care budgets shrank in the 1980s and 1990s, doctors were instructed to spend less time with their patients in order to see more patients in a day, thus increasing productivity and maximizing profits. I had this experience myself when I was practicing within a conventional setting. At first, I was able to spend an hour with each new patient. By the end, I was allowed just 15 minutes, and even this is above average. Doctors now spend an average of seven minutes with each patient, often interrupting patients within seconds after they begin talking.

There is no way that such a brief consultation could provide a doctor with enough information to make a well-informed diagnosis or devise an appropriate course of treatment. In many cases, the doctor has little or no previous knowledge of the patient, making the whole experience even more of a guessing game. Naturally, this scenario does not instill confidence in a patient.

Feeling unheard and uncared for within a conventional medical setting, many patients began exploring other forms of treatment. Their dissatisfaction was a catalyst for the move away from illness-based care to well-ness-based care. The result was increased interest in complementary and alternative medicine, known collectively as CAM. Recognizing the growing popularity and use of unconventional medicine, Congress passed legislation in 1991 funding an office within the National Institutes of Health (NIH) to investigate and evaluate complementary and alternative medical practices. Two years later, the NIH established the Office of Alternative Medicine. By 1998, the office had become an official NIH center and was renamed the National Center for Complementary and Alternative Medicine (NCCAM). Today, NCCAM takes a lead role in documenting the effectiveness of CAM, advancing research in the field, and disseminating information to the public.

Every five years, the National Center for Health Statistics' annual National Health Interview Survey contains a section on CAM. The most recent available statistics show that approximately 38 percent of U.S. adults aged 18 years and over and approximately 12 percent of children use some form of CAM. The most common CAM therapies among adults are natural products, deep breathing, meditation, and chiropractic and osteopathic. These therapies were most often used to treat musculoskeletal problems such as back, neck, and joint pain. The overwhelming majority of patients use CAM as part of a complementary approach, where it accompanies, rather than replaces, conventional medicine. These individuals spent more than $33 billion out-of-pocket on CAM practitioners, products, classes, and materials.

One of Dr. Weil's teachings I took to heart was to focus on a patient's healing. In medicine, a modality refers to the therapeutic agent, usually physical, used to treat a patient. Examples in conventional medicine are chemotherapy and surgery. Alternative modalities might include acupuncture or homeopathy. Dr. Weil taught us that as physicians, we should detach themselves from particular modalities or therapies and opt for what best serves the patient. The terms "alternative" and "complementary" are not simply about modalities. Any modality can be used in either an alternative or complementary manner. I believe that by examining each situation thoroughly and mindfully, we increase the possible benefit and decrease the possibility of adverse reactions.

This brings us to integrative medicine, the form of medicine I now practice. The NCCAM defines integrative medicine as that which "combines conventional and CAM treatments for which there is evidence of safety and effectiveness." Dr. Weil's Arizona Center for Integrative Medicine defines integrative medicine as "healing-oriented medicine that takes account of the whole person, including all aspects of lifestyle. It emphasizes the therapeutic relationship between practitioner and patient, is informed by evidence, and makes use of all appropriate therapies." The center's definition also encompasses the following principles:

1. Patient and practitioner are partners in the healing process.
2. All factors that influence health, wellness, and disease are taken into consideration, including mind, spirit and community, as well as the body.
3. Appropriate use of both conventional and alternative methods facilitates the body's innate healing response.
4. Effective interventions that are natural and less invasive should be used whenever possible.
5. Integrative medicine neither rejects conventional medicine nor accepts alternative therapies uncritically.
6. Good medicine is based in good science. It is inquiry-driven and open to new paradigms.
7. Alongside the concept of treatment, the broader concepts of health promotion and the prevention of illness are paramount.
8. Practitioners of integrative medicine should exemplify its principles and commit themselves to self-exploration and self-development.

As these statements demonstrate, integrative medicine emphasizes openness, scientific evaluation, collaboration, and inclusiveness. Going beyond the bounds of complementary, alternative, and holistic medicine, integrative medicine has become a growing force within conventional medicine. More than 50 U.S. and Canadian medicals schools and teaching hospitals now incorporate integrative medicine into their curricula.

While conventional medicine reduces the body down to its component parts—lung, heart, nervous system, etc.—integrative medicine, in the tradition of holistic medicine, takes into account the whole person, recognizing that a human being is a complex, interdependent system and that the system as a whole has properties separate and distinct from the properties of each individual part. In integrative medicine, an examination of the whole extends to exploring a patient's spirituality, emotional state, relationships, and behaviors. It also takes into consideration a wide variety of treatment and care options that may be used alone or in combination.

As a physician and a proponent of integrative medicine, my role is to be a guide in helping my patients find solutions to their medical problems. Both conventional medical resources and alternative modes of healing are used in the context of a healing partnership. It was Dr. Bernie Siegel who led me to the acknowledgement that people are spiritual beings experiencing a human journey. This philosophy of making spirituality the center of healing is what we practice at Georgia Integrative Medicine. During my practice, I have been fortunate to witness the power of healing that comes from mending relationships with the inner self, higher self, and other selves. People feel they are more "whole." Healing and being present in the moment are so very important because death, the natural consequence of life, awaits us all.

CHAPTER 4

MAPPING THE PATH

The way forward seems to lead back.
Tao Te Ching

When I left Arizona, I had a deeper understanding of where my interests lay, and a more focused idea of my destination. However, I had yet to map the route. I was still searching for a way to realize my vision.

We returned to California, where I had been offered the position of dean of integrative medicine at the Acupuncture & Integrative Medicine College, Berkeley. The college made an active effort to integrate modern Western medicine with the ancient traditions of Chinese medicine. My experiences were positive overall; I was able to build a successful integrative medicine program and the work environment was ideal. Yet I felt unsure of my role within the organization and I sensed my calling more strongly than ever: to bring integrative medicine to the mainstream.

A new opportunity presented itself when I was recruited to run an integrative care facility on the outskirts of Atlanta, Georgia. This required another family upheaval.

This time, it was not an easy transition. My son had become attached to friends and family in California and was reluctant to move. After the relocation to Georgia, Vena found it difficult to juggle childcare and work. To make matters worse, it soon became clear that my expectations did not align with those of my new employer, and it became impossible for me to continue in the position. Rather than compromise my principles, I decided to leave.

The author Franz Kafka wrote, "From a certain point onward there is no longer any turning back. That is the point that must be reached." For me, that point of no return came in 2007. Finding myself stranded in Georgia without a job was the most difficult challenge of my life. I had uprooted my family and moved across the country, only to find myself unemployed and with no immediate prospects. Our financial resources were limited. It was then that the seed of an idea began to take root. It was not, in essence, a new idea, but one that had been percolating for years.

I began to realize that every degree, training course, and certification I earned had brought me to this place. I feel fortunate to have found Georgia, but in truth, Georgia found me. I came here hoping to serve people and to create an organization where integrative medicine could flourish. Things did not proceed the way I had anticipated, but the vision was not lost. Maybe this was the opportunity I had been waiting for all along.

My experiences in academia and in the private and public sectors gave me a broad perspective. By this time, I had studied and worked in the field of integrative medicine for years. I had developed several clinical programs in integrative medicine, including one full-scale operation. I also had firsthand on-site knowledge of many integrative medicine programs where I was able to observe what works and what doesn't. After visiting close to a dozen clinics, I realized that all of them had an integrative medicine mission, but were still driven by a conventional structure and a profit motive. Furthermore, they neglected the welfare of their employees. I could see that the status quo was not good enough. Integrative medicine needs to be housed in an integral organization, an organization that redefines the role of employee-employer and does not simply function as a mainstream corporation. Again and again, I found myself asking the same question: "How can the system improve?"

Lessons learned from Dr. Weil proved useful. I saw how he had created a community of supporters. I remembered his observation that the first step in a revolution was to create a counterculture, to create a community with values that run counter to the culture. The mission became clear. I would create a community of healers to provide comprehensive integrative medicine in a collaborative setting. Our organization would be based on integrity and what author Stephen Covey termed "true north" principles. These include fairness, kindness, dignity, charity, integrity, honesty, quality, service, and patience.

If the goal was clear, the logistics were not immediately obvious. How do we create community? How does it function? It is one thing to have a gathering of like-minded people. It is another to sustain healthy, well-rounded relationships among multiple people for an extended period of time while providing productive services (in this case, healing) to people in need. Anyone who has ever been part of a family or a conventional workplace of any size—in other words, almost all of us—will understand the difficulties inherent in human relationships. Entrenched dysfunction is a hallmark of many workplaces. This is especially unfortunate and counterintuitive when you are trying to help people improve health and maintain wellness.

For myself, the road to understanding the power of community began with a search for my true self and the realization that there are three relationships each one of us must seek to nurture:

1. A relationship with one's inner self.
2. A relationship with one's higher self.
3. A relationship with others.

The relationship with our inner self involves gaining a working understanding of our character and habits, and making a commitment to evolve our consciousness. Of course, in-depth work on this level can be never ending. Zen practitioners spend their entire lives in search of "true self." Some find meditation techniques such as Transcendental Meditation or Mindfulness Meditation helpful to develop insight and grounding. Others use reading, reflecting, and writing as a way to elucidate their inner natures. Still others spend time in nature to help to develop a connection with their inner selves.

One commonality of inner self-development is that only the individual who is seeking to form that relationship can achieve it. He or she may have assistance in many forms, including counseling or a teacher's guidance. However, knowing oneself cannot come about simply through reading other people's ideas or listening to them. Self-knowledge is attained as a result of introspection. This is not always an easy or straightforward endeavor. Sometimes when we take that journey, we might not like what we find. Facing uncomfortable truths about ourselves and seeking to improve is part of the process.

The relationship with a higher self involves identifying and following true north principles. Although many people use a specific religion to guide them in a relationship with the higher self, some people utilize a more eclectic approach focusing on spirituality. For example, Gandhi committed to the principle of non-violence as a means to win independence from the British Empire. There are also countless Native Americans and Taoist mystics who simply chose to exist in the harmony of nature.

The relationship with others is an outward manifestation of the first two relationships. I believe that in order to serve others, one needs to be grounded. Too many leaders fail in their mission to serve others because they have not succeeded in establishing relationships with their inner selves or with a higher self.

It would have been futile and foolish to even contemplate pursuing my vision without the support of the person closest to me: my wife, Vena. Since we met in high school, she has been the most powerful influence in my life, teaching me about the power of softness, honesty, and timing. I feel fortunate to be living with someone who has more expertise than I in the Tao and Te of relationships. I am constantly learning about subtleties of the Way and the power of relationships by observing Vena's interactions with people.

When my son was born, a mentor told me that living with him would be like living with a Zen master. He was right. My son, like children everywhere, is especially adept at finding the right buttons to push and he takes great pleasure in doing so. He has taught me the value of mindfulness and of keeping my actions firm, fair, and consistent. Furthermore, his continued growth means that I need to adapt continually to keep up with him.

Relationships demand consistent and constant attention. In the practice of tai chi I find helpful reminders about how to foster a harmonious relationship. The principles of tai chi include mindfully exercising softness, listening, and yielding, all skills that need to be maintained by constant practice. In a relationship, it is inevitable to encounter stressful situations. If we can approach these situations with an ability to listen, an attempt to understand, a willingness to yield, and a soft reaction, it is likely we can enhance and strengthen our relationships over time.

As fate would have it, Vena also faced professional challenges when we moved to Georgia. Although she was able to find a job, maintaining a balance between work and family was problematic. Trying to work full time as well as manage our son's schedule became impossible. She proposed a work-from-home arrangement, but it was not approved. The situation was frustrating, but again, what appeared to be a calamity was in fact an opportunity. Anyone starting an organization, whether for profit or not, needs help with the money: banking, budgeting, payroll, accounts payable and receivable, on and on. Here was someone with financial expertise, extensive experience, and irreproachable ethics, someone whose philosophy and values mirror my own. The community was already taking shape.

We had the substantial advantage of owning a house in a live-work community that supports residents who wish to work where they live. This allowed me to begin my practice at home. Unbeknownst to me, I had already begun to form the external relationships that would lead to the creation of our team. Having left my job, I was on my own to create a space in which to work and practice. I no longer worked for anyone else, but was free to work for myself. And yet I was not alone.

As a result of working diligently, I had built a strong foundation within the local community. When I made the decision to leave my job, a group of more than two dozen people, mostly patients and tai chi students who felt they had benefited from my assistance, met to discuss how they could keep me in the area. This support was priceless, and demonstrated the need for the kind of services I was hoping to provide.

The feeling of liberation that comes with following one's calling cannot be overstated. I believe everyone is an artist and his or her life reflects the art. Too many people are limited by their perception of reality, and as a result they find themselves trapped in jobs by steady pay and benefits rather than pursuing a vocation based on their true calling or interests. What is worse is that we often encourage the young to pursue a "respectable" career whether the career suits them or not. As a result, there is a massive epidemic of unhappiness in our society. This malaise in turn manifests itself in the form of addictions, psychological problems, and even in chronic illnesses. Part of the appeal of creating a community is that it provides a chance to help others realize their own potential while doing the same for myself.

From the outset, my intention was to create a space for integrative medicine that was different from all those I had previously observed. The integrative medicine facilities I visited all had one thing in common. They were institutions based on the American corporate model. Although they were attempting an innovative kind of medicine, they were doing it within the same conventional context used by mainstream medical institutions. So while the techniques were new, the structure was not.

When I reflected on how I might do things differently, the teachings of Jesus came to mind. In a parable detailed in the Book of Luke, Jesus tells his disciples:

No one tears a piece out of a new garment to patch an old one. Otherwise, they will have torn the new garment, and the patch from the new will not match the old. And no one pours new wine into old wineskins. Otherwise, the new wine will burst the skins; the wine will run out and the wineskins will be ruined. No, new wine must be poured into new wineskins. (Luke 5:36-38, New International Version)

I knew I wanted to do things completely differently, to craft a "new wineskin." First and foremost, I wanted to create an environment in which people were valued not merely for their labor, but as individuals. The automotive pioneer Henry Ford once famously asked, "How come when I want a pair of hands I get a human being as well?" The idea of workers as cogs in a machine may have originated with the Industrial Revolution, but it has endured well into the 21st century. Despite technological advances that allow us greater mobility, speed, convenience, and ability, as Americans we continue to work under conditions that dehumanize and devalue us. Employees are often viewed as dispensable and interchangeable. Much is asked of them and little given in return. Job stability is practically nonexistent, and with the economy still in recovery, those who are able to get jobs consider themselves fortunate, whatever the drawbacks may be.

This mentality is not conducive to physical, psychological, or emotional wellness. We know that when we are stressed, angry, resentful, or experiencing any negative emotion, it is difficult to focus on anything else. If we are not well ourselves, how can we hope to help others maintain and improve their own health?

As an integral organization, our mission is not to return the highest return to shareholders, but to create the highest good for our employees and our patients. This means helping team members to grow and giving them the opportunity to express themselves in ways that draw on their varied strengths and talents.

This is counterintuitive to the conventional approach to hiring, in which an employer creates a job description and finds someone to fill it. Imagine the typical job interview, in which the candidate tries to customize his or her experience to meet the requirements of the job, whether or not it truly fits.

I have had the experience of trying to conform to convention. I worked for large organizations. I understand what it is like, even as a physician, to be a cog in a machine. The difference is that instead of auto parts moving along an assembly line, our health system has patients moving through an exam room. And when a manufacturer discovers it has made a mistake, it can recall the vehicle. When we miss something with a patient, the implications are much more serious, potentially fatal.

Jon Ronson, author of *The Psychopath Test: A Journey Through the Madness Industry*, cites a study showing that the incidence of psychopathy among corporate leaders is four or five times higher than in the general population. Given that one of the traits of a psychopath is a lack of empathy, this is an interesting comment on modern corporate America. Some executives believe that creating an adversarial environment within the workplace is good for business, that by encouraging a survival of the fittest atmosphere, the company will thrive. This is a destructive, shortsighted, and inhumane approach.

My philosophy of leadership takes a different tack. I have mentioned Art, my medical school professor who taught me a great deal about being a servant leader. Robert Greenleaf popularized the phrase "servant leadership" in his 1970 essay, *The Servant as Leader*. In the essay, Greenleaf, who worked for AT&T for nearly 40 years, proposed that a servant-leader is one whose first desire is to serve. Leadership follows as a consequence of that desire to be of service. A servant-leader looks out for the well-being and needs of others, supports their development, and shares power and decision making. This differs from the traditional structure of leadership in which there is one person at the top wielding power unilaterally. The concept of servant leadership itself is not new. It can be found in the pages of the *Tao Te Ching*:

> *The sage acts for the people's benefit; he trusts them; he leaves them alone.*
>
> *Working, yet not taking credit; leading without controlling or dominating.*
>
> *One who heeds this power brings the Tao to this very earth.*

The truth is that this form of leadership is not only altruistic; it is the most productive way to run an organization. This is in essence the whole point of the *Tao*. When we behave in ways that are true, honest, and right, it makes everything better. This is true for us as individuals. It is true with regard to our interactions with others, and it is undoubtedly true in the workplace. If we treat people with compassion and understanding, they will be motivated to do their best. Fear, greed, and other negative emotions can also serve to motivate, but they often produce unreliable results and create even more problems.

This is not to suggest that it is always easy to do the right thing. As you will see in later chapters, creating an integral organization is the first phase. Sustaining it is an ongoing process. Just as a garden needs tending and nourishing, so too do people.

When I first arrived in Georgia with my family, I could never have imagined that we would end up where we are now. In fact, when I first began to realize that the position I had been recruited for was untenable, there were moments of real despair. Throughout my career, there have been other moments of tension when my natural instincts and principles have come into conflict with external forces. But abandoning a steady paycheck is not something done lightly. And this time there was nothing waiting for me on the other side.

Of course I was mistaken. What awaited me was the culmination of all the highs and low I had been through. My younger self would not have been ready to embrace this kind of challenge, but I had finally reached the stage in my life where I was ready to apply all the principles, knowledge, and lessons I had learned. I had Vena by my side, and all that remained was to seek out the other members of our community.

Unbeknownst to me, I had already found them. This endeavor would have been impossible without the dedicated individuals who were critical to building the infrastructure of the clinic. They form the core of the community I envisioned. Jeanne, Nola, and Dorothy, all of whom I met while still working in my previous job, were to join us in creating Georgia Integrative Medicine. Their stories are as much a part of Georgia Integrative Medicine as mine is.

In the beginning, we faced the same difficulties as any new company. We started out in my home, but we could not stay there. We had the enthusiasm and the passion, but operations, marketing, IT, finance, and team building—these were all equally important. We overcame each challenge by applying tai chi principles. The principles of relaxing and grounding and yielding and redirecting helped us survive the "Great Recession" which started about the time we opened our doors at the present location.

In the following chapters, you will discover how the clinic became a reality, how it functions, how we interact, and how we practice both good medicine and good business. It is an unusual model, but I believe that our work serves as an example of what can be done when empowered individuals come together to improve the common good. In that sense, it should have universal appeal, not just for those interested in healing, but for anyone seeking to bring about constructive change in the world. For us, change begins at the basic level of physical and emotional health.

PART II: THE PEOPLE

道

INTRODUCING THE TEAM

I was confident in my vision for a clinic and in my own ability to practice integrative medicine, but bringing the dream to fruition would not have been possible without the individuals whose stories follow. I have asked them to tell the stories in their own words so that readers are able to understand the process from multiple perspectives. This is in keeping with our method of working, which incorporates opinions and input from each team member. From the outset, collaboration has been an inherent part of our mission, and it continues in these pages. In each case, the story ends with my own thoughts about the person's contributions and qualities.

We operate in a world that values productivity, quantity, and efficiency over effectiveness. This example is clearly demonstrated in today's mass production approach to medicine. The antidote to this is medicine that values a therapeutic healing partnership between patients and physicians.

My greatest blessing in coming to Georgia was to meet my team members. I have done my best to serve each of them by encouraging a balance of personal and professional growth. I consider myself extremely fortunate in the relationships I have enjoyed over the years. First and foremost is the relationship with my wife Vena, who has also become a colleague. The first story is hers.

Jeanne's story follows. She serves as the clinic's manager and director of operations, and oversees mind-body medicine. After that, we hear from Nola, who directs our food as medicine program. Her specialty is homeopathy. Finally, Dorothy shares her story. Dorothy has been both a patient and a volunteer at the clinic. As you will discover, each of these individuals plays a role that goes far beyond simple job titles. We have all been together since the clinic's inception and they each bring unique, essential qualities to the table.

Chapter 5

VENA

I joined Georgia Integrative Medicine seeking balance between work and family. After we moved to Georgia, I was unable to find a job that allowed me to manage both work and childcare in a satisfactory way. This caused me anguish. When I was invited to join Georgia Integrative Medicine, it was the beginning of a very different work life for me that ultimately not only afforded me a fulfilling work/life balance, but also blessed me with the love and support of the clinic community.

I began by doing work for them on the weekends. With my accounting background, I was able to set up QuickBooks for the company and deal with the finances. When I transitioned to a full-time position, my role was chief financial officer (CFO). After a while, my position expanded to include chief executive officer (CEO) duties. In that capacity, I oversee the financial and administrative details of the organization.

Previously in my career, I had worked in big companies. I was in accounting and Securities and Exchange

Commission (SEC) reporting departments that had strong team support. SEC reporting, in particular, relied heavily on teamwork and togetherness because there were times we spent eighteen consecutive hours with one another as we worked to meet reporting deadlines. Looking back now, I realize that the unity we had then was due to the nature of our jobs. I was very fortunate to have great supervisors who always looked out for the needs and well-being of each team member. However, from the corporate perspective, we were just employees, and therefore dispensable.

As a small business, Georgia Integrative Medicine doesn't have the financial power of a big corporation. On the other hand, because we're so small, everyone is important. After I joined the clinic, I began to realize the true level of synergy we have here. We are not just employees, but friends who truly care about and enjoy spending time with one another. Not only have I found a job that allows me to balance my life and work, I have an extended family to support me and help raise my child.

Since joining Georgia Integrative Medicine, I have lost two loved ones. The first was a parrot that I had for sixteen years. As soon as Jeanne heard of the parrot's death, she dropped what she was doing to come lend me a shoulder to cry on. Later, she signed us up for belly dancing class as a way to help me cope with the loss and to bring some joy back into my life.

The second loss was the passing away of my father in 2011. The entire Georgia Integrative Medicine community swooped in to take care of my family and me like a mother hen. My father really suffered the last two months of his life and he finally passed away peacefully in my home. During home hospice, Dorothy and her husband, Bill, came daily to take care of my father, tending to his every need. For the love and compassion they showed him, I am very grateful. The night before my father passed away really made me realize what an amazing and loving community we have. Nola showed up at the house, saying God had told her to come because my father was leaving soon. Then one by one, everyone gathered at our home, even though it was a Sunday night. Dorothy and Bill took care of my father and stayed with him until the end. They called the hospice nurse in charge and waited for the funeral home to come and take him away.

Although this is the most supportive community I have ever worked in, initially it was not easy for me. When I joined the team, I knew my career had to take a back seat in order to ensure my child's emotional needs were met. Since my husband and I previously made equal financial contributions to the household, it was difficult for me to feel financially dependent on him and to feel like my career was railroaded.

In addition, I had never worked for a start-up before. The challenges of starting a business and keeping it going were unlike anything I had ever experienced. There were times when we all had to sit together and brainstorm strategies to keep the doors open, including the possibility of letting one of us go. Yet every time such an issue came up, we always chose to all take pay cuts before letting someone go. Such choices are unheard of in a typical business, where the decision to hire or dismiss is usually made by the immediate supervisor or owner of the business, not by community consensus.

In most business settings, employees are disposable assets because they have to fit into their jobs and are hired for the skill sets they bring with them. Therefore, when someone leaves a job, another person with similar abilities can fill that position quite quickly. At Georgia Integrative Medicine, however, employees are first and foremost integral members of the community and cannot be replaced so easily. In fact, the team really does function like the parts of a clock. Any one missing or malfunctioning part creates such a disruption that the rest of the team is adversely affected. So, it is not easy for us to ask people to leave.

Conversely, we are very particular about who becomes part of the team. We have to get to know them and see if they fit in. If we don't get along, at some point something will invariably happen that causes more problems. Everyone must agree on the person coming in. All of us have to give our input. Generally, team members are chosen for their commitment to healing and their passion for what GIM does. We then create the job skills according to aptitude and interest. This process requires an extended period of getting to know one another.

Because we operate differently from a conventional business, we cannot follow the conventional trajectory. It's not a matter of setting an expansion goal and steaming ahead. If we don't maintain a delicate symmetry, things will fall apart. If and how we grow depends on the people we meet and whether they fit into our team. These elements are out of our control. We cannot predict when we might find the right person. Consequently, our focus is really on our own well-being. We have to take care of our resources and people are the most valuable resources we've got. Of course we want to take good care of our patients, but we can't do that if our providers are burned out.

When people are indispensable, the natural thing to do is to take care of them. Georgia Integrative Medicine's unique way of doing this is through sharing tea and in-house meals. At teatime, my husband usually serves all of us and we use the time to stay connected. Over tea, we not only address business issues, but also discuss anything we would like to share with one another. Often, it is an opportunity for us to relax and enjoy one another's company when there is down time. It is a way of "feeding our souls."

Nola takes care of feeding our bodies. She prepares gluten-free, dairy-free meals for us. She makes all of us happy just by smelling and anticipating our mealtimes. Again, participating in shared meals helps us to grow as a community. Lunchtimes are intentionally longer than at most other businesses so that we cannot just enjoy the good, nutritious meals, but enjoy one another's company and relax.

For years I've been telling my husband that he is a trendsetter. There are not too many people practicing integrative medicine the way he does. Most people do it in a disjointed way. At GIM, everybody's talents go into taking care of one patient. Most other clinics don't do that. As a trendsetter, the hardest thing is waiting for people's mindsets to change. And they are starting to change. Traditional medicine is great for emergencies, but it is a Band-Aid to health care. If you have symptoms, you are given pills, but what about the side effects of the pills? Mainstream medicine works to suppress symptoms rater than to target the root of the problem, which is what we are trying to do.

There is an awful lot of togetherness in the GIM community. Due to this closeness, I can say we work in an extended family setting rather than a strictly professional setting. Yet, somehow, it really works. It is a healing environment not only for our patients but also for every one of us on the team.

About Vena

We are very fortunate to have Vena in our community. Most companies of our size do not have a dedicated Certified Public Accountant as a full-time team member. At first, she joined as an accountant. In two years, she became our chief financial officer. Today, she serves as chief executive officer.

Vena brings with her strategy and business processes from large corporations. What makes her a treasure is that she administers with an efficiency, kindness, and fairness that I have not yet seen in the corporate world. Vena is often referred as the "fair wise judge." We regularly consult her when there is a disagreement between two of us, and we abide by her decision. She is trusted and loved by all of us. I almost get the feeling that my team members tolerate me, but they love Vena unconditionally.

Vena is one of the quietest and most unobtrusive team members. Yet she is a warm, loving person who checks in on everyone, sits and offers insights into difficult challenges, solves financial problems, and always exudes a calm wisdom with her presence. My offer to Vena was that she come and goes as she pleases as long as the company is doing well and the books are in order. However, I noticed that she does not take advantage of our arrangement. Most times, one can find Vena sitting beside the receptionist's chair greeting patients and listening to their stories while working on the accounts or analyzing the finances. Most patients have no idea that they are talking with the chief executive officer of Georgia Integrative Medicine.

Vena's decision-making process always supports the idea that the clinic has to have a heart and soul and warmth. It can't be cold. This means that she is always trying to make sure we operate with a conscience and that whatever choices we make for our employees or for our patients comes from the heart.

Vena has taught me the importance of compassion and justness. She rescues animals, among them two dogs, two cats, and two parrots. Her qualities have helped our company to do the right things for our patients and our team members. Sometimes, these acts of kindnesses have resulted in financial losses, but she says that creating te or virtue is good for business, and I think she is correct. Being compassionate allows our team members to feel that we can work morally while still creating a strong business.

Vena has also been trained to perform as a medical assistant, lifestyle educator, and energy medicine practitioner. I do not expect her to perform clinical functions. However, it is important that as part of the leadership of a health care organization, she understands the demands of frontline work so that when she makes a command decision, she is able to relate to the clinical team's needs. In most corporations, I noticed that there is a chasm between the frontline workers and the boardroom.

In short, Vena represents yin energy. She is quietly observing, listening, and gentle while my leadership style is more yang energy—quick, active, and direct. I feel fortunate that our talents combine well and I am able to provide strategic leadership while she and Jeanne manage the everyday running of the business.

Chapter 6

JEANNE

My extensive and varied work history began at the age of 13 when I cleaned stalls and fed horses to earn the privilege of having my own horse. By the time I was 18, was married with a baby to support. My older sister guided me into the legal field as a secretary. I went to work for a small law firm in Atlanta and by the time I was 22, I was in one of the biggest law firms in the southeast, making a good living.

At the time, I did not think then about evolving consciousness or mission or purpose. I thought only of doing my work, going home, and getting paid. Like most others, I was focused on survival and making a living to support my family. I did not stop to think about whether I enjoyed my employment, and though I met many wonderful people during more than 25 years as a legal secretary, I cannot really say we formed a sense of community.

In 1988, a traumatic event in my family led me to enter therapy with a psychiatrist and social worker. Both of them commented on my natural aptitude for therapy and said I should consider it as a career. I liked the idea, but it felt impossible to me. My occupation as a legal secretary was safe, secure, and financially rewarding. It wasn't until my psychiatrist broached the subject again that I began to consider it seriously. I asked myself, "Why not?" And at the age of 37, I quit my job at the law firm and enrolled at Mercer University to pursue a bachelor's degree in human services.

I completed an internship at Inner Harbour Hospital, a psychiatric facility for troubled youth, and ended up staying for five years, which felt like the equivalent of twenty years' worth of experience. I had several friends there with whom I bonded. We were working in a highly volatile environment. You could say that we were bonded by the trauma we encountered on a daily basis. We had to be hyper vigilant to keep our patients safe, but also to protect one another. In that respect, we did have a sense of community. We had meaning and purpose in our work and felt it was an important, if low paying, job.

Still, working under these extremely difficult conditions took a toll, and after the five years, I returned to the law, finding a position in a small law firm that allowed me to recuperate and recharge. I was at that firm for nine years. During that time, I had another therapist ask me when I was going to go back to school. Again, it was the nudge I needed, because I immediately started the ball rolling on enrollment at the University of West Georgia to earn my master's in psychology.

JEANNE

Looking back now, I can see that a series of puzzle pieces were moving into place. A good friend of mine had been in an automobile accident. Her physical therapist was also a tai chi teacher. My friend asked if I would go to tai chi class with her. At this point, I weighed 230 pounds and was in terrible physical shape. I still had my health, but no stamina. I had always struggled with my weight, but during the time I worked at Inner Harbour, I comforted and anesthetized myself with food. I survived this intensely emotional job by meditating, journaling, and eating. I totally ignored the fact that my physical body was part of the equation until the day when my lab results came back and my cholesterol and thyroid were both out of control. I saw a word on my chart that was the rudest of awakenings: "OBESE." Then I had to pay attention. I had to take action.

My initial feeling was that my body had betrayed me. It took me some time to learn that my body was only trying to get my attention so that I would come to understand and assimilate a whole picture of health. Tai chi sounded perfect to me, as it was a gentle, meditative way for me to move and simultaneously engage in spiritual activity. It was a two-for-one in my mind. It was a non-threatening activity and did not strain my cumbersome body. Tai chi helped me make friends with my body once again. In order to be truly healthy, I had to re-integrate the physical into my way of being. If I wanted to be empowered, healthy, and whole, I had to understand that my body had a mind of its own.

As time went on, I found myself enjoying my body, and soon, yoga, walking, hiking, and biking became part of my physical regimen. I even took up belly dancing for fun. I decided I wanted to become a personal trainer and pursue my master's in psychology so that I could marry personal training with psychotherapy. I lost 50 pounds and began to feel at home in my body for the first time in my life. I had been able to stabilize my weight by maintaining a regular schedule of exercise and following a low glycemic food plan. However, when menopause arrived, it announced itself by joining with my hypothyroidism and insulin resistance (a precursor to diabetes). The result was inevitable weight gain, despite my strict exercise regimen. I began to panic. Feelings of hopelessness and despair came over me. My doctor prescribed a diabetes medicine for my insulin resistance, but nothing worked. Before I knew it, I had regained 28 of the 50 pounds I had lost. When I pressured my doctor for help, he told me that since I was eating right and exercising, there was nothing else he could do for me and that I would just have to accept the fact that although I was fit, I would always be fat. The medical model was useless. I did not know where else to turn.

I was completing my master's degree and teaching a weekly tai chi class when a friend suggested I contact Dr. Kim. When she persisted, I wrote him a long email about how I believed emotions contribute to sickness and about my idea of starting a business combining counseling with personal training. He wrote back one line: "Come have tea with me."

Eventually we met for tea and spent more than an hour conversing, although I don't remember talking much. He said, "Some people are just curious, and I can guide them. Others want to learn, and those I teach. You are about transformation; it is what gives you joy. You, I will teach." The other thing he told me struck me squarely in the solar plexus. When he asked me if I was seeking licensure as a counselor, I responded that I wasn't sure what I wanted to do. His words hit me with a blast of truth. "Of course you should seek licensure. A license gives you power. The only thing stopping you is that you don't think you are good enough for it." Ouch.

When I left our meeting, I wasn't sure what I had agreed to, but I knew that I had to do it. I had performed psychic readings on the side for a while, and when I spoke to Dr. Kim, he did to me what I'd been doing to everyone else all those years. I felt he saw right into me. He was able to tell me all about myself. It was reassuring and frightening at the same time. I felt exposed, but also recognized and acknowledged.

We started slowly. I took Tuesday afternoons off, thanks to my extremely cooperative boss. I observed Dr. Kim's work with patients and joined him in teaching tai chi. After observing his compassionate therapeutic manner with patients, I decided to ask him for help with my weight gain. I poured out my frustrations and he looked at me and said, "Oh, that's easy. It's just biochemistry. I can help you with that." In the 50 years I had struggled with my weight, never had I heard the words, "I can help you with that." The burden had always been on my shoulders, mine to tackle alone. Now here was some-one telling me it was no big deal, he could help me. According to him, it was really quite simple. With tears in my eyes, I thought, "Where do I sign up?"

I bought my supplements and within the first few days felt a dramatic difference. Once my blood sugar stabi-lized, I felt good at levels I did not know existed. I real-ized that I had been suffering from a low-level agitation to which I had become so desensitized that I had been unaware of its presence. Now I felt light, happy, and hopeful. Weight began to fall off effortlessly. My crav-ings disappeared and it became easier to eat healthy food. My taste buds became less dictatorial and I be-came attuned to my body's nutritional needs. You see, it was never really about the weight at all; it was about my consciousness about weight. Stabilizing and balanc-ing my body chemistry gave me clarity and insight and made it possible for me to let go of the need to lose weight and instead focus on health and wellness. Once my consciousness made the shift from "losing," the threat was removed and there was room for me to gain what mattered most to me: health and vitality. People began to comment that I looked younger. Indeed, I felt that I was aging in reverse. I had recovered my joy.

Jeanne

I'm not exaggerating when I say that I believe that Dr. Kim is the best doctor in the world. He is a visionary, far ahead of the times. I speak from experience—not only mine, but that of my husband Stanley. For many years, I watched him crawl around on the floor in pain after a fishing or hunting trip because his ankles were rubbing bone on bone. His foot and ankle specialist informed us there was nothing he could do except fuse Stanley's ankles together. This doctor was not at all enthused about this option and explained that Stanley would not only lose flexibility, but would likely still wind up in a wheelchair in five years. For Stanley, ankle fusion would be a last ditch intervention to keep him on his feet for a few more years.

I asked Dr. Kim if there was anything he could do. He answered that Stanley's condition was perhaps too far along for him to help, but that he was willing to try. Stanley was skeptical, stating that he couldn't see how acupuncture would help him with arthritis pain. He was resistant to trying at all until his back went out and Dr. Kim was able to treat his back pain, getting immediate results merely by using auricular acupuncture. This impressed Stanley enough to sign up to give arthritis treatment for his arthritis a try.

Dr. Kim started Stanley on an anti-inflammatory regimen paired with weekly acupuncture. It was slow going at first, but after six weeks, Stanley's biochemistry had changed and the pain that he had suffered with for many years began to disappear. The first thing I noticed was I did not hear him moaning and groaning in the mornings when he got up. He just stood up and walked to the bathroom without any difficulty. As long as he is consistent with his supplementation regimen, his pain is managed easily. The wheelchair his specialist predicted looks like it might have to wait. Stanley tells anyone who will stand still long enough to listen about how Dr. Kim has improved his quality of life.

Dr. Kim and his integrative medicine saved me from diabetes and all of its complications and kept my husband out of a wheelchair. It is as simple as that.

When Dr. Kim decided to start his own clinic, he suggested that I meet him at his home for a daily early morning nature walk before I headed downtown to work. This meant waking up two hours earlier every day. At first I thought he'd lost his mind, but something propelled me, demanded of me that I do this thing, and I did it. Each day, I rose at 5 a.m. and walked with him until 8:30, then went to my job and worked all day. I did not know it then, but Dr. Kim was observing my level of commitment, my ability to invest in discomfort to gain a new way of life.

With family help, I was able to secure myself financially so that I could take a one-month leave of absence to undertake an internship with Dr. Kim. On my last day of work at the law firm, I told my boss, "I'll see you in month." He said, "No, you won't." "Don't you want me to come back?" I asked. "I want you to be happy," was his reply. Two weeks later I told him that he was right, that I was not coming back. Dr. Kim and I were going to build a clinic together in Tyrone, Georgia.

On one of our walks, Dr. Kim told me that he needed me to organize his office and help with the clinic. He also said that he could not pay me any more than he paid himself, which was minimum wage. How could I possibly manage that? Somehow I did. I could not understand why Dr. Kim wanted me, someone with a long way to go to become a therapist, when he could find licensed therapists growing on trees who would love the opportunity to work in an integrative medicine setting. His response was, "Skill sets I can buy. The right people are much more difficult to find." It turns out I was the right person, and he was willing to wait for me to hone my skills.

Since then, we have built more than an integrative medicine clinic. We have built a community of healers and patients who work together toward one common goal: providing health and wellness in integral ways. I work as the clinic manager, lifestyle educator, and mind-body practitioner. I earned my master's degree in psychology and my transformation continues. Bringing tai chi practice into everyday life means that I am mindful of the traps of fixed consciousness, and each day I am filled with gratitude for the energy Dr. Kim has invested in his own education so that he can be of service to the rest of us. I am filled with gratitude, hope, and humility and eagerly face each day as an opportunity to be of service to our patients. If I can give back a fraction of what has been given to me, it will be more than enough to balance the scales.

It is very difficult to describe the sense of community we share. It really has to be experienced firsthand, but I will do my best to explain.

Imagine a place where the chief executive officer, chief financial officer, and chief operational officer gather at payroll time, look at what funds there are, and then decide what the payroll will be for that period. Imagine flexible payroll, where the employees voluntarily take pay cuts to help the company stay afloat in hard times. Imagine a company where the employees feel they are all in one big lifeboat rowing together, looking for ways to conserve and expand.

Imagine working in a company where an employee can call on any one of its officers, day or night, for help. Imagine a company where it is more important to take a break, sit down and connect with one another, than to keep busy working and producing. This latter idea may be a bit harder to swallow. American industry focuses on production. In most companies, breaks and lunch hours are set at specific times, and there are often-times consequences for going over these time limits, which may include docked pay, write-ups, and possibly termination.

At Georgia Integrative Medicine, we start each day with a team meeting. "How was your weekend?" "How are you today?" We ask these questions before we start in on our workday. And if one of us needs time to talk about anything at all, that comes first, before work. We operate this way because we understand that we are not our work, we are complex individuals. What American companies do not comprehend is that people bring their complexities to work. We know that as humans, we have issues, hurts, and hopes, all of which come in the door with us each day and are bound up in the work we do in the clinic. So we connect and we prize the time together. It is the backbone of what we do to keep our company running.

Dr. Kim demonstrates intense interest in each one of us personally and professionally. He is always looking for ways to improve our situations. I have had very good bosses in the past. I have been fortunate. But Dr. Kim takes it to another level. Dr. Kim says, "Show me where the Jeanne tree is so that I can go pick another one." This reminds me that my attributes, personality, characteristics, and experience are very special. There is only one of me and Dr. Kim reminds me on a daily basis that I am a treasure. It is the same for anyone who joins our team.

We were told early on that we would have to work very hard for the first five years, and we did. We worked upwards of seventy to eighty hours a week. As much as I would love to give everything I have to make us successful, we recognize the natural aging process and the need to practice what we preach to our patients, which to take better care of ourselves. If we were to do things the traditional way, I would be allowed to work myself into illness, then I would have to quit, and the company would hire a replacement. Our team recognizes that we must love, conserve, and protect one another, to build for the future.

I've never worked anywhere where people worried so much about me. It takes some getting used to. They ask me, "How are you? What's going on in your life?" If we don't have clarity in our lives, we're going to bring that to work with us. Healing starts from the first contact with a patient on the phone. They need to feel healing energy when they walk in the door. Healing is going to be disrupted if there's conflicting energy coming from us, so when we do have conflict, we iron it out right then and there.

Dr. Kim says, "Jeanne, without you, there is no Georgia Integrative Medicine." What he means is that none of us are expendable. That is different from any other environment in which I have worked. I have been highly valued, yes, but I have never been reminded so frequently that I am irreplaceable, that I am a valuable, integral part of the team.

I said earlier that I had grown twenty years in the short five years I counseled troubled youth at Inner Harbour. The years I have been with Dr. Kim, working side by side as a team member, have been the equivalent of eons in terms of what I have learned about myself, about how to be human, how to build relationships, about sustainability and truth. The winds that blew me here were the biggest blessing I could ever have asked for, and I will continue to let those winds of change lead me as they help me transform and stay fresh and whole.

About Jeanne

Jeanne is an amazing person. She had a job with wonderful benefits, a considerate boss, and a good salary. She gave up financial security to take a minimum wage job at a risky underfunded start-up venture called Georgia Integrative Medicine that had no guarantees and no benefits. She believed in a vision and pursued it. I am very grateful for Jeanne's trust.

In return for her leap of faith, Jeanne got the opportunity of a lifetime: to pursue her singular path. I believe that everyone has a gift. I feel that as the director of Georgia Integrative Medicine, my job is to assist team members in advancing their healing potential without harming themselves. Jeanne completed a master's degree in psychology and she is currently in the process of obtaining a licensure in professional counseling. Every aspect of Jeanne's life has more balance. I notice that she is more at ease with herself, her spouse, and patients.

I am most impressed by Jeanne's willingness to learn, her can-do spirit, and her complete belief in our mission. Even when things look bleak and impossible, Jeanne's faith and strength carries the community.

Jeanne was shocked that I was willing to wait ten years for her to complete her master's degree, a post master's degree as an Education Specialist (EdS), and the Georgia state licensure requirements for professional counseling.

Unlike most companies that seek to fill a position, Georgia Integrative Medicine is on the lookout for the right person. The right person must have a calling and a mission to serve. That right person can be trained to pursue the mission they are called to perform. However, the person with right skills may never develop a true passion and therefore, may never fit in with our community. Over the years, we have retained all of our core team members. Even the retired members remain as volunteers. The fact that we have a retention rate of almost 100 percent despite the fact we pay lower than most companies is a paradox.

JEANNE

Whereas most companies begin with a job description, at Georgia Integrative Medicine, a job description is created for each individual based on interests, strengths, and passion for excellence in healing. For example, Jeanne loves mind-body medicine, reflexology, and counseling. Therefore, her job revolves around activities she loves. This way, she will feel as if her work is her play.

Jeanne serves as the clinic manager, sales manager, and chief operating officer because of strengths in her character and her zeal for the mission and vision of the company. Probably the most difficult challenge she had to overcome was the mental shift around leadership. As a legal secretary, she simply followed her lawyer's lead. Here at Georgia Integrative Medicine, she has to be proactive. That means taking initiative, thinking for oneself, and devising the best solutions. Often, it is more difficult to find the best solution than to follow rules blindly.

I feel privileged to guide, observe, and serve Jeanne in her journey at Georgia Integrative Medicine.

CHAPTER 7

NOLA

When I met Dr. Kim in 2006, I was working as a corporate executive chef. I cooked and was also involved in wellness programs and helping people with nutritional issues. Dr. Kim and I met through a mutual acquaintance. We discovered that we shared a love of tea sharing and we began to have tea together. After he struck out on his own, he asked if I would like to work for him one day a week. As I was contemplating the offer, my company went through restructuring and I was told my services were no longer needed.

I prayed about what to do next and received the answer to go see Dr. Kim. Unsure, I prayed again to muster the courage to act. Finally, I drove over to his home office and Dr. Kim answered the door. As it happened, his receptionist had quit that very day. I felt as if God had orchestrated it perfectly so that I could take this new path.

We started with one treatment room, Dr. Kim, Jeanne, and I. We all had a lot of growing and learning to do. We weren't sure of how we were going to work together, but right away we started building our community, sharing time and space, our dreams and ideas for what would become Georgia Integrative Medicine.

My particular interests and training were in nutrition and homeopathy. I've been helping people my whole life with nutrition and food, using herbs. When my youngest child started school, I enrolled in the nutrition program at Georgia State. After that, I was able to practice naturopathy. Right after I started back at school, I inherited some books from a friend whose father passed away. A couple of the books were on homeopathy, and I began studying them. Although I had a deep interest, I was still in the beginning stages of training. Dr. Kim funded my education so that I could obtain a diploma and a certificate in homeopathy and a certificate in nutrition. As a start-up venture, we did not have enough funds to pay for the courses. He borrowed the money so that I could pursue my dream.

My first experiences with homeopathy involved family members. When my son's arm was itching badly from poison ivy, I gave him a remedy and it went down to about half the size. By the end of the second day, it was all gone. Not long after that, my mother called me and said something was wrong with her eye, some kind of hemorrhage. She had gone to the ophthalmologist, who told her not to lift anything heavy. Well, she had to lift heavy boxes as part of her job. She asked me what I could do. By then, I had gotten a remedy medica, which is a reference guide for homeopathy. I was able to give her a remedy and by the next day, the blood had disappeared.

I went on from there, studying and attending conferences. Now I serve as Dr. Kim's main medical assistant. I also do the homeopathic intake. I'm looking for patterns and ways that a person reacts to things, how they eat, how they sleep, the kinds of cravings they have. Mostly what I do is listen and observe. A case well taken is 90 percent of the job. I let people talk and I can get most of what I need from what they say. I'm trying to pinpoint where the dysfunction is and what it is that needs to be healed. In homeopathy, the premise is not to treat the illness. It's about treating the person. This is even the case with acute illnesses. You can have five people who have the flu and have five different remedies. It depends on how they express their symptoms and where their dysfunction is. Similarly, you don't treat depression. You're looking for where the patient is out of balance and treat that. Homeopathic remedies are made from mainly from plant, animal, and mineral sources.

With my background as a chef, I also help all the people who come to the clinic for food as medicine. Most illnesses that Americans experience today are derived from inflammation. Conventional medicine originated in a period when illness was not associated with inflammation. It came from diseases like tuberculosis and all the other infectious diseases that killed people. We rarely work with infectious disease at our clinic. Conventional medicine is not good at dealing with the chronic illnesses we see. People end up on lots and lots of medicine. The more medicine that you take, the more side effects you have. This is especially true when people are older and are going to multiple doctors: the cardiologist, the urologist, etc. The doctors don't talk to each other and people get in trouble.

The kind of medicine we are practicing is very much on a case-by-case basis. Most people feel like even the case taking is beneficial. I don't always end up giving people remedies. I had one patient, a lady in her 80s who had severe anxiety. When she came to us, she couldn't walk. She was in a wheelchair. She had a lot of anger inside of her. Her oxygen level was very low and she came to get acupuncture to help her breathe. I took her case and she told me about her mother. Her mother was not nice to the kids when they were growing up and as a result, this woman had become hardened. She also had a very tender sweetness inside, but she retained a lot of anger about her childhood. When I took her case, she cried and said, "You don't know what this means to me. I have never told anybody about these things."

To me, it was such a blessing and an honor to be there for her. She stayed with us for quite some time. She had such a neat, wonderful soul and a week after she got her remedy, she was talking to her nephew. He was amazed at how she'd changed, and he said, "What happened to you?" We often see that people are lonesome and they want somebody to listen to them.

Music is another big interest of mine. My first degree is in music and I play the violin. For a long time, I suffered from stage fright. I see similarities between my musical life and my work as a homeopath. When you play music with other people, it's the same as when you take a case in homeopathy. You need to be on your toes. You have to observe and adjust.

Dr. Kim asks, "Is this your first day working here?" He encourages me to approach patients with a "beginner's mind." This is a Zen concept that refers to keeping your mind open, ready, and compassionate, free of biases and assumptions. In homeopathy, you have to always go in with a beginner's mind. It helps in all the work we do, because you can't go in with preconceptions—for example, a patient may have Parkinson's Disease, but that doesn't define the person.

I don't get stage fright anymore. These days, I find it easier to play with a musician I've never played with before. I have to listen very carefully. Similarly, I find it easier to take the case of someone I don't know. In fact, it's harder to be the doctor for people in your family. There's less clarity. When you see somebody for the first time, the things that stand out help you to see what is needed.

What's most rewarding for me is when people start feeling better. We often review our patients' cases and evaluate their progress. We are constantly looking for efficacy in treatment. How long did the treatment last? Are they getting better? When we see that improvement, it reassures us that we are doing what we're supposed to be doing.

I remember about six weeks after Dr. Kim began teaching me tai chi, I went kayaking one afternoon and suddenly realized that my technique had improved dramatically. What had changed? I came to the conclusion that the lifting hands opening movement in tai chi had allowed me to learn to relax my shoulders. Guiding the kayak was no longer that struggle against the current. I was now able to glide gently through the water, no longer forcing the paddle, but gently pushing the water to work with the current. What an amazing day that was, full of peace and grace.

I also realized that I began to feel that I am in the place where I ought to be, doing the work I should be doing, with the people I am intended to be working with. In a most intimate way, we are given the opportunity to listen to people's stories, and give them a safe place to cry, to laugh, and to explore the possibility of healing and wholeness. I am far from completing my journey. On the contrary, there is still so much to learn, so much of this great mystery of life. I have received so many blessings, and endured great hardship, all of which

God has allowed me to put to use in some way to ease the burden of others. My youngest son recently asked me why I changed careers so many times. I told him it's because I needed the experience I gained along the way to arrive at the place where I am now, so that I could accomplish the task set before me. I have learned to be quiet and even to be still, and sit with myself, sometimes not liking what I see, still seeking direction. God blessed the broken road that led me here to this place and time, and I am so glad to be here.

About Nola
Nola is an amazing person. She possesses a rare gift that combines patience, love, and hope. She also has mastered the power of prayer. Nola functions in so many roles at Georgia Integrative Medicine. She cooks for the team members and guests, she educates patients on how to use food as medicine, and she works as my medical assistant.

Among Nola's many gifts, the most precious gift may be her genuine love for people and her ability to listen to them. I have never met a better listener than Nola. I have observed her doing a better job of listening than patients who are professional counselors.

Nola had many difficulties in the beginning due to her lack of a medical background. Whereas Jeanne and I have both worked for hospitals and worked with licensed professionals, Nola had diverse work experience, but had not worked in a licensed professional medical environment. As a result, many lessons had to be learned on the job through trial and error. But she has overcome these hurdles with equanimity, acceptance, and faith.

At Georgia Integrative Medicine, we look at the person as a whole and try to understand that person as well as we can. That process, unfortunately, is quite slow and deliberate, taking place over several years through the sharing of many cups of tea and lunches. What I first saw in Nola was a diamond in the rough. Nola is still maturing as a professional. It may take another decade to complete that evolution, which means that we will have invested more than 15 years in her development. Most human resources directors would consider me out of my mind to spend so much time nurturing one employee.

From my perspective, the people I love are the most important resource in the world. I view them as gift from God and see myself in the role of steward. Because of my belief that team members were entrusted to me by God, I feel that my responsibility is to help them become the best healers they can be.

There is a corollary to this approach. In certain people, it inspires loyalty, which is very rare in American companies these days. It engenders trust in my leadership, which is crucial, especially as I have to take financial risks moving forward. Team members trust that I know what I am doing and that the outcome will benefit all of us. They believe, rightly, that I have their best interests at heart.

Chapter 8

DOROTHY

I first came to the Georgia Integrative Medicine community as a patient, although I am also a registered nurse, certified in Neonatal Intensive Care with a master's degree in adult education. I practiced nursing for more than 30 years.

I found the clinic after a life-changing auto accident. In May 2004, my husband and I were involved in a high speed rear-end collision. The force of the impact shattered the rear bumper on my side, and caused the metal frame of the tire well to shatter 360 degrees in all directions. The rear of the car was picked up and jolted through the intersection, which caused it to lurch forward and backward, breaking the seats of the car. When the tail of the car hit the ground, I landed on the metal between the seat cushions. I experienced a blinding white light from the pain that shot up through my spine to my head. The pain was a sharp, throbbing, burning sensation and my hands tingled from mid-arm to my fingertips. I felt as though a sharp object was jabbing me at the base of my spine.

Diagnosed in the emergency room as having severe muscle strain, I was prescribed heat, rest, pain medications, and muscle relaxants, and told I could return to work in 48 hours. For two months after the accident, I participated in physical therapy (PT), took medications, and continued to work as a nurse. After six weeks of PT, I underwent an MRI due to worsening of pain and impaired movement from severe muscle spasms. In addition, I had burning and stabbing needle-like pains all over my body. I was unable to sit, stand, or lay down for longer than 15 minutes at a time. I feared the worst: permanent back injury, disability, and the loss of my job and career.

I began monthly injections that consisted of having needles and catheters placed in my spine. Four months after the accident, I had a severe lack of mobility in my large intestine. While dealing with strong laxatives to correct this side effect of my medications, I required emergency gallbladder surgery. According to the pathologist's report, the gallbladder had been badly bruised on the right side during the accident, causing it to cease functioning. I continued with PT and pain management techniques, but my pain was so severe that I was eventually referred to the "premier" pain clinic in Atlanta. Unfortunately, there was a two-month waiting period. Not satisfied with the progress I was making and debilitated by worsening pain, I requested a medical leave of absence from work. I was exhausted and unable to concentrate. Even the act of talking was painful. I was not able to hold a phone receiver without my mid-back going into spasms.

My pain medications continued to escalate in dosage, I suffered from severe nausea, sweats, all over burning, muscles that felt hard as rocks everywhere I touched. It seemed my body was being compressed from all sides in an unrelenting vice. I could not stand a fan or air conditioning or even the bed sheets touching my skin. It set them on fire.

I kept my appointment with the "premier" pain clinic, which resulted in two of the most painful examinations of my life, after which the head of the clinic told me, "I don't think I can help you. I can send you to physical therapy with a specialist, but other than that, there is nothing I can do for you." I cried uncontrollably. I had waited two months for this "holistic, comprehensive pain service" and was rejected as untreatable. I prayed for relief, for someone who would know what to do to help me become pain-free again.

Not only was it becoming impossible to carry out my life's work, but there was also the reality of lost wages, lost productivity, lost friends, lost job, lost movement, poor attention, sleep disturbance, fatigue, irritability, and impaired mental and physical functions. Maintaining stamina and clarity of focus were a huge challenge. I even experienced a loss of direction and self in the process of navigating the health system, lawyers, and insurance. Declining mobility compounded my misery. My mind, body, and spirit were all struggling. The pain was killing me and I wasn't even sure I had received an accurate diagnosis.

In addition to all these pain-related issues, I also had diabetes, which I had managed through diet and exercise before the accident. I was gaining more weight due to the medications and limited mobility. At the same time, I was also experiencing a rare side effect of my cholesterol medication. It was damaging the muscles in my legs and arms. Stopping this medication reduced my pain in my legs tremendously and probably saved my life.

I share my medical history to illustrate the extent to which I had exhausted conventional medical options. My husband and I had been to more than 185 provider visits in the two and a half years prior to visiting Dr. Kim. This includes hospitals, physical therapy clinics, pain clinics, neurologists, neurosurgeons, massage therapy, biofeedback, prolotherapy, medical acupuncture, visual imagery, you name it. I've experienced firsthand the good and bad side of Versed, Darvocet, Flexeril, Soma Compound, Ultram, Demerol, Morphine, Oxycontin, Phenergan, Reglan, and other medications. I weathered two surgeries, a total of 12 injections in the spine, 23 prolotherapy injections in the back and sacral joints, three years of physical therapy, and 34 sessions of medical acupuncture. Life has been a roller coaster ride of improvements followed by flare-ups of increasing pain.

Dorothy

Life looked pretty dim. I had spent my entire professional life trusting and working beside many excellent
health care providers. My heart was broken, my life as
I knew it was gone, and needless to say, my financial
health faded as well. The suffering continued to inten-
sify. The system knocked me down, beat me up, and
essentially threw me out the door as hopeless.

I chose to check out a referral to Dr. Kim at the end of
2006. As a nurse, I was impressed by the comprehen-
siveness of his integrative medicine exam. He looked
at all of my medication and set me up with an anti-
inflammatory, low-glycemic meal plan that would control my diabetes. He put me on multiple supplements
to help control glucose levels. These changes brought
everything back under control.

Then he saw that the pain itself wasn't being controlled
well and he began treating me with acupuncture, using
multiple approaches. I eventually stopped seeing all
physicians except for Dr. Kim. Over time, he was even
able to wean me off all medications.

The answer to my prayers came in the form of a talent-
ed spiritual physician and teacher. Dr. Kim said, "There
is only one word I want you to think about… GRACE…
nothing else, and relax, let your body heal itself; get out
of its way." Those words rested on my spirit like gold,
and I knew God had provided the help I had always
believed was out there.

Dr. Kim's strategy was simple. He said, "Mrs. Carey, you are an RN, are you not?" I responded that I was. He continued, "Are you a good nurse, Mrs. Carey?" I replied that I was an excellent nurse. "Good," he said. "Mrs. Carey, I want you to meet your new patient, Miss Dorothy. I'm counting on your good nursing to take care of Miss Dorothy."

Suddenly, I became the most important patient of my life! There began the journey we must all take, the one of caring for self. By pushing myself and trying to force healing, I had prevented my own recovery. I've learned to relax and let nature take its course, be patient and kind to myself. As nurses we are taught to have non-judgmental attitudes toward our patients. My personal experience with suffering has taught me non-judgmental attachment: acceptance of the experience as just that, an experience to observe and from which to learn.

I began to practice tai chi, which taught me how to connect to the earth, to cultivate my energy, and be present. Previously, I was so busy "doing" to get well that I forgot about "being." Learning to forgive myself for failing to heal within a specified textbook timeframe helped me release a tremendous amount of self-induced pressure. I didn't have to be perfect. I just had to be myself and relax in God's grace and love while my body naturally healed itself.

Dorothy

Dr. Kim invited me to participate in an internship at the clinic, which was an honor. I learned more about integrative medicine and a lifestyle of prevention and wellness. I continued to do that until I finally decided to retire and focus on taking care of myself. I continue to do what I can behind the scenes and am involved with training and compliance issues at the clinic.

Unique is a good word for the experience of being a team member at Georgia Integrative Medicine, but it doesn't fully describe it. What makes this group so unusual is their inspirational love. It is an indescribable power of togetherness manifested in the hearts and minds of all who participate in the community. As a patient, feeling this power motivated me to heal a broken body, a weary mind, and a wounded spirit.

They were there with me in my pain and fear, sensing my heartbreak and suffering. They were there holding out their arms to embrace me with a healing love like no other medical community had ever done. The connection we established provided me with a renewing energy that allowed me to heal.

Dr. Kim believed he could help me even when experts in conventional medicine told him that they didn't think it was possible. He had the dream of creating a great healing community. I was blessed to be one of the first patients at the home practice that would grow to be Georgia Integrative Medicine.

Back then I was in a lot of trouble with severe chronic pain. I was pouring sweat, barely able to walk into the office. With each treatment, I was one day closer to a new life. I felt Dr. Kim's dedication, his creativity, his compassion, and sincere love for me as a fellow human being. That love fueled my determination to heal. Think about having a doctor who truly loves you as a person and believes in your capacity to heal! Well, I was blessed with that gift. Along with this special physician came a new team of providers who are still with him today: Jeanne and Nola.

Dr. Kim, Jeanne, and Nola are the heart of Georgia Integrative Medicine. The synergy they create as a team of healers is unmatched. In the typical medical office, one enters a waiting area full of people reading magazines, staring at a TV, or making sure no one sits next to them. At Georgia Integrative Medicine, you open the door to smiling faces that are glad to see you. They ask about your life, share their stories, and keep you company while you have a short wait. You don't see that kind of treatment from a typical medical team. You're not just a number.

In the back office, you are greeted with that same smiling love as they continually check in on how you are doing. It doesn't matter how busy they are, they always have time to sincerely connect with you, a rare gift in a medical setting. They create a community of supporters who walk on a healing journey with you, a loving community where you feel safe and assured that whatever your state, healing is possible.

Dr. Kim's compassion and tenacity are perpetual gifts; he is either inspiring you with his love and dedication or "poking" you (as we call it), challenging you to greater self-awareness and actualization. It isn't all fun, but it is all for our total well-being. Leading each patient and team member to his or her full potential as a spiritual being is part of the integrative approach to healing that he practices.

At Georgia Integrative Medicine, mind, body, and spirit are tended with loving care for each soul present. The clinic offers an array of services, including food as medicine, lessons on how to prepare food in healthy ways, medical supplements to boost healing, herbal medicine, acupuncture, tai chi, mind-body tools, and multiple healing systems.

No other medical environment will offer you the change to participate in tai chi with fellow patients as you learn not only the art of movement meditation, but about balance, strength, and relationship management alongside your physician and treatment team. Rare is the physician that will gather the team in a patient's room to hold a prayer circle for that patient. The power that this type of community brings to their acts of healing is unsurpassed.

A few patients have become team members through their association with Georgia Integrative Medicine. The team decides who will fit into their group. Prospective candidates include the many volunteers who are there to support the staff. Skills are important, but fit is paramount. One must be able to integrate into the community in a balanced way and share the vision of changing health care one patient at a time. The individual must be able to show a willingness to suffer hardship and inconvenience in order to become a team member.

What is it like to be a team member? Well, have you ever had your boss sit down and serve you exquisite Chinese tea in a ceremony designed to spend time with you and honor your special nature? Have you ever had a leader say, "We will find a way to make it work?"

I had the opportunity to join the team on a training trip to Florida. Because my body perceives pain differently, I told Dr. Kim I couldn't do it. If I walk more than 20 minutes, the pain kicks in. He told me he had arranged for me to have a scooter so I could be part of the team. We visited Epcot Center and they walked alongside me as I rode the scooter. What's more, they picked activities that they knew would bring joy to my spirit, even though they had already experienced them.

The value that they place on my life and on me as a human being is such a rare gift. There are no words to truly express what it means to me. When one of the team has a difficult life challenge, everyone is there to support and serve that person, not because they have been asked to, but because it is what they do naturally from their hearts. When one team member is absent because of an illness, he or she receives medical assistance, food, and attention from the rest of the group.

I've watched Dr. Kim research and propose simple and workable solutions to problems when they arise. Joint sacrifices are made to keep the organization viable. His leadership, resourcefulness, and persistence in being there for his team are what make this such a great community. His team members are there for him and each other as well. But it is the loving human spirit that resides in each of us that makes this group distinctive and special.

About Dorothy
Dorothy has been a keen observer of our community at Georgia Integrative Medicine. As a patient and volunteer, she had a rare opportunity to observe us from within. Along with Jeanne, Dorothy has made a tremendous positive impact on my practice and on my personal growth as a person and a physician. She has been integral in helping to guide and train other team members, always giving generously of her knowledge and time.

Vena and I have become close friends with Dorothy. Vena spoke of how Dorothy and her husband Bill helped to take care of my dying father-in-law in his final days. From patient to volunteer to friend, Dorothy has demonstrated compassion, expertise, and the "loving spirit" she describes. As someone who nursed others with tender care for so many years, we are grateful to have her as part of our healing community.

Chapter 9

SUPPORTING MEMBERS

In addition to the core team members, others have contributed to our work throughout the years. Some continue on with us today. Others have moved on. Even if they are no longer with us in an official capacity, their experiences are valuable in understanding what we do. Here are a few of their stories.

Stanley

We often talk about how the team at Georgia Integrative is like a family, and Stanley is a literal example of this. As Jeanne's husband, Stanley has also been involved with us from the beginning. At his wife's encouragement, Stanley came in as a patient, and as Jeanne describes in her story, received treatment that allowed him to remain mobile when he had been told he was headed for a wheelchair.

Like many people, Stanley has worked hard his entire life. He spent almost 20 years working for a company where he was exposed to the elements, long hours, and extremely stressful work. These conditions understandably took a toll on his health. Despite the hardships, he persevered. Then one day, after giving years of his life to this company, he reported to work only to be told that the owner had sold the business.

When I learned that Stanley had lost his job, I was worried. I could see him slipping into anxiety and depression. I knew that his chances of finding a new job were extremely low, given his age and health and the general state of the economy. I felt we faced a potential catastrophe. I was concerned that Stanley would not survive this forced retirement. I think lack of purpose and meaning in life is very harmful to one's soul. I see many men who become ill and die shortly after retirement. Men who prepare for a healthy retirement do much better.

I knew that it would be immoral and unethical to watch Stanley silently suffer the consequences of his situation. I also knew that if anything happened to him, Jeanne's health and welfare were also at risk. So, I created a position for him answering phones and managing inventory. Even though it was financially very tricky to add another employee, I viewed it as an investment in in both his and Jeanne's wellness. There were some adjustment issues. Having worked in the field and warehouse, working indoors was initially tough for him. However, he was a wonderful host to our patients, receiving and engaging them in lively discussions or telling stories.

One of Stanley's most important contributions came in the form of thoughtfulness. Jeanne had told me of his kindness towards animals, but I did not expect that benevolence to extend to our patients and team members. It was like having an elf performing all the important work behind the scenes without claiming any credit. He performed random little acts of kindness for everyone in the clinic. For me, it meant that I could always count on having enough water to serve tea. He bought coffee for the coffee drinkers, nuts and fruit for the team members, and he washed sheets for the clinic.

When he reached 62, Stanley retired happily. His retirement is turning out very differently than it might have because he planned for it. Today, Stanley still volunteers for the clinic and I am very grateful to him for his generosity.

Tempie
Tempie is one of our volunteers and my tai chi student. We describe her as a gentle rain in a drought. She comes into the clinic every week to perform non-medical tasks. Her contributions allow the rest of the team to focus on healing and also provide her with a sense of fulfillment. As she says, "What I do makes me happy, brings me joy, a positive focus in my life each week—and, unexpectedly, has provided me with a sense of belonging within the wellness community that is Georgia Integrative Medicine."

I've mentioned the "clinic with a soul" quality that Vena has been instrumental in promoting and nourishing.

Tempie calls this "a warmth that surrounds even when the day is over—an afterglow from being in the presence of caring people."

PART III: THE PRACTICE

道

CHAPTER 10

CREATING THE SPACE

If there is a good store of virtue, then nothing is impossible.
Tao Te Ching

Although our community is special, we are by no means perfect, and the clinic is not a utopian paradise. We are human beings with flaws and foibles, just like everyone else. The difference is that we make a daily conscious effort to interact harmoniously with one another and to keep focused on our shared mission and on one another.

From the beginning, I set out to create an environment that promotes harmony and values people as individuals while maintaining cohesion within the group. As director, I have to be deliberate in my actions in order to keep us on that track. This necessitates continual monitoring of the dynamics within the clinic, the behavior of each team member, and the general atmosphere and appearance of the space. Is everything in equilibrium? If not, where are we off balance and how can it be corrected?

Relationships

Establishing and sustaining healthy relationships is the most important life skill that is not formally taught. From birth, we are creating bonds with people that will shape our experiences and perspectives for a lifetime.

In the *Tao Te Ching*, Lao Tzu writes, "Where the mystery is the deepest is the gate of all that is subtle and wonderful." Viewing relationships as a deep mystery speaks to their intricacy and helps to remind me to keep a beginner's mind in my daily relationships. Taking someone for granted and being taken for granted are sure ways of eroding bonds. Over time, relationships can deteriorate until there is no emotional content left, often leading to a loss of the relationship and great suffering.

In our community, the influence of relationships, both internal and external, cannot be overstated. The way we relate to one another, the way we relate to others in our lives, the way we relate to our patients, and the way our patients relate to people in their lives—these connections impact health and healing in a profound way.

In our relations with others, it is easy to fall into habits that become difficult to break, to follow patterns that are dysfunctional, but familiar. The thought of moving ourselves out of these negative relationship ruts and into something healthier and more positive can often feel overwhelming and scary.

When I first met Jeanne, I told her there was one thing I wanted her to do. I asked her to work on her relationship with her husband, Stanley. They had been married for many years and had reached a level of complacency with their relationship, which was not ideal. Jeanne called Stanley "the mountain that cannot move." When I asked her to work on the relationship, she said, "Anything but that!"

Practice of the Tao and the cultivation of Te do not imply that one will become perfect. Rather, it produces a mature perspective, where you can view viewing failure as a form of feedback, which gives you an opportunity to engage in continuous improvement. Just as I try to continually improve my relationships and psychological and physical health, I ask team members to do the same.

My advice to Jeanne was to be tender to Stanley, and she was. She was tender in a mindful way and worked very hard at "moving the mountain." What she discovered in the process was that Stanley wasn't immoveable. It was her perception of him that had become fixed. Once she understood that and realized she had the power to change, everything was different. Stanley and Jeanne have been married for nearly 40 years and survived the tragic loss of their son. If they had not worked so hard to strengthen their relationship, the marriage may not have survived that tragedy. Stanley makes a concerted effort to tend to Jeanne's needs and they enjoy one another's company. She says that their relationship is better today than it has ever been.

It may seem strange or even shocking for an employer to ask an employee to work on his or her marriage, but what we are aiming for with our community is something far removed from what is "usual." My observation is that the qualities one exhibits in a primary relationship will likely emerge in other relationships in daily life. Therefore, if my primary relationships are not harmonious, what hope do I have of sustaining healthy working relationships with co-workers?

It is all about what contributes to the common good. Does it help if you have a relationship where your husband is yelling at you? Is it helpful when there is tension between you and your children? How are your relationships helping you or hurting you, and by extension, helping or hurting your colleagues?

People only change when they want to and when they need to, so I wait. I wait until the external issue creates a problem at work. If it causes a disruption, I feel free to talk about it and discuss how it needs to be corrected. For example, a team member's child was always leaving his musical instrument at home, and she had to leave work repeatedly to retrieve the instrument and deliver it to him at school. This began to have an adverse effect on the clinic. If a problem is significant, sooner or later it will seep into the workplace.

In criminology, the "broken windows theory" posits that if we do not address problems when they are small, they will soon escalate into something much more serious. For example, if a window on a building is broken, that is a relatively minor issue. However, if it is not repaired, the vandalism will continue and grow, leading to theft, and worse. Similarly, if someone has a problem at home that is not addressed, it will continue to fester and eventually the person will find it affecting his or her work, interfering with healing, and potentially endangering a patient. This is something we have to guard against.

Relationships are not only significant for team members. They also play a vital role in healing. One of our patients, on her first visit to the clinic, said, "I am afraid if I get well, I will have to divorce my husband." The fear of breaking up her marriage represented a major barrier to healing for this patient. However, she was able to achieve a level of healing without losing her marriage. This was achieved by practicing mindfulness in her relationship with her husband. She learned to be assertive in her relationship and began to state her needs clearly to her spouse. Because of the emotional work she put in, her body was able to heal synergistically. Her initial statement about her fears helped our team to be alert and cautious throughout her treatment.

These examples emphasize not only the importance of healthy relationships, but also the detrimental effects of unhealthy relationships. The types of relationships we perpetuate are symbols of how we feel about ourselves, how we value ourselves, and how we relate to the larger world. I see the potency of relationships in healing every day. The dynamics are complex and powerful.

One man who was dying of cancer lamented, "I just wish my wife would touch me."

In his final days when all he wanted from her was comfort, all she could do for him was to "take care of business." Too much had happened and the breach between them was too deep and too wide. He was too weak to make the leap, and she was unwilling to reach out to him. Another woman with cancer was more afraid for her husband than she was for herself. Each patient has a relational story that is an integral piece of the healing puzzle.

People come to Georgia Integrative Medicine seeking help for a number of conditions, including anxiety, depression, chronic pain, multiple sclerosis, cancer, arthritis, stress, diabetes, hypertension, addiction, and myriad of other physical ailments. But they arrive with more than physical concerns. They bring their hopes, fears, dramas, and pain. What kind of medicine do they seek? They seek a compassionate ear, a caring heart, and a loving touch. They seek a community of intuitive healing and a team of professionals who are invested in them. One patient summed it up aptly when she said, "You are in the business of touching souls here."

Integrative medicine has its foundations in building healing partnerships with patients. Without the ability to form these healing partnerships, we would become like any other allopathic clinic, spending a few minutes with each patient and writing prescriptions. Instead, we take the time to connect and forge a relationship.

To facilitate the patient-healer relationship, each member of our clinic is asked daily to (1) be present; (2) tell the truth; and (3) detach from the results of telling the truth. We are called upon to be dedicated to our internal work so that we can be mindful of and present in our own human condition, focused on how to connect and serve, and open to learning more about how to stay committed to our mission.

Integrative medicine is about the relationship of mind, body, and spirit for each patient; it is about the interpersonal relationships in the patient's life; it is about our relationship with that patient.

Through our relations with others, we have the power to influence them for better or worse, depending on our choices. For each person who chooses to enter into a lifelong process of learning, self-actualization, individuation, awakening, transcendence, or whatever term best suits, others in that person's life are affected one way or the other. The strength of our choices to learn, grow, and evolve can inspire those around us.

Tea Sharing

"Tea is nought but this: first you heat the water, then you make the tea. Then you drink it properly. That is all you need to know."
Sen Rikyu

"If you asked me the secret ingredient to our success, I would say two words: tea sharing."
Jeanne

I first became familiar with tea sharing as a ceremonial activity when qi gong Master Ken Cohen took me to his favorite teahouse in San Francisco, where he introduced me to Roy, a tea master who helped me acquire an appreciation for the art.

I chose to integrate tea sharing at Georgia Integrative Medicine for many reasons. It helps to build team unity, promotes bonding, and provides an opportunity for me to serve my team members. At first I used the phrase "tea ceremony," but it sounded too formal. "Tea sharing" has a much more down-to-earth ring. We have tea sharing several times a day, if we can, whenever we have time, or if patients are late or don't turn up. Where other medical clinics would choose to spend those lulls catching up on work, we prefer to catch up with one another.

My office serves as a tearoom. Anytime someone wants to have some tea, he or she can come in. It's a time for us to interact with one another and deepen our connection. We discuss patient cases and ask about each other's lives. By providing a social setting within which to share moments from our lives, tea sharing promotes communication. The tearoom is where we can resolve conflicts and tend to our harmony, as one would tend to a garden. But it is also our time to relax, rest, and rejuvenate. We've done a great job getting to know each other, so much so that we may know each other better than we know the families we grew up with. Tea is also useful medicinally. If a team member comes in upset, I might invite her in for tea and choose a variety that helps to calm nerves.

The ritual itself is an abbreviated form of a Chinese tea ceremony, although we use tools from Japan and Korea as well. The tea is always medium to high quality. No one should have to suffer through bad tea. I'm the boss, but by serving tea, I am embodying servant leadership. When your boss asks you to have tea, it's easier than having to seek permission to enjoy that period of stillness or respite. Tea sharing is a great teambuilding experience and differentiates our clinic from other medical offices. We sit at a round table to foster an environment of equality where everyone can speak freely.

This openness is vital in a setting where we must work together in service to our patients. Georgia Integrative

Medicine is a comprehensive integrative medicine clinic offering many modalities, including Western medicine, Chinese medicine, homeopathy, naturopathy, and mind-body medicine. We are outcome driven, which means we do our best to focus on a patient's outcome rather than on what technique was used in treatment. Sharing tea several times a day helps to engender trust and respect among team members.

Obtaining the best water for tea, heating the water to the correct temperature in order to bring out its optimal taste, brewing the tea for right duration, and serving it properly—all these steps take time, effort, and mindfulness. Even though I have served tea several times a day, 300 days a year, for the past ten years, I still find a lot of room for improvement. This is a reminder to me that we can always find ways to better our relationships, team development, and the treatment of our patients.

For me, teatime is an opportunity to be focused and mindful. As the host, I have to be on guard. I observe each person. Are the cups empty? Are the cups not empty? If someone's tea cup gets low, I refill it until I am told the person has had enough. Spending time together this way allows me to stay alert to what is happening with the team. Many people have spoken of the synergy we enjoy. Our success relies on a harmonious balance between differing personalities, amidst the stresses and strains of everyday life.

Small details often provide insight into the larger picture. If vessels from yesterday are not cleared away, I know the team is off, and we need to take action. This is our early warning system. If we have issues within the team, before long we'll have issues with patients, and that's unacceptable.

I do not enjoy confrontation. However, since I am extremely sensitive to disharmony, I prefer to endure the discomfort of early intervention in order to preserve harmony in the long run. At Georgia Integrative Medicine, if one member complains about another member in his or her absence, I find a time for the two people to connect and provide an opportunity to bring up the concern in the presence of both individuals. I find that I rarely have to repeat this practice.

Chinese medicine espouses the concept of Five Phases or Five Elements, which can be used to refer to everything from the natural world to medicinal properties. The phases or elements are: earth, fire, wood, water, and metal. We use the phases in our medical practice, but we also use them to understand one another. The phases can be used to illustrate the personalities of each team member.

Jeanne is earth-fire. For earth people, the number one priority is loyalty. Her enthusiasm and passion can be seen as fire characteristics. These qualities are useful in helping her bring in new patients and guiding them in the right direction. We don't rely on hard sell techniques or coercion. We simply explain who we are and what we can do for each prospective patient. We want people to come here willingly and leave happy.

Nola represents an earth-water combination. Water people are more reticent and cautious. They play their cards closer to their chest. Whereas Jeanne has no secrets and makes her thoughts known, Nola tends to keep her thoughts to herself. Vena is earth-metal. She has the warmth and compassion of an earth person, but also the high ethical moral standards of a metal person. As she demonstrates regularly, she is always going to be fair and non-judgmental. I am a wood-fire combination. Wood people are highly creative, ambitious, and visionary, but there is also the element of fire, which contains the passion and energy. Jeanne will tell you that we tend to clash because we both reflect fire traits.

Thinking of one another in this context helps us understand one another better because we recognize that we are inherently different. When we act the way we do, it's not because we're trying to be difficult, but because that is who we are. We each have something distinctive to offer because of our relationships to the elements and how our personalities reveal themselves in interactions with other people. Metal and water play it safe. Earth and wood jump in at the deep end. Diversity is an advantage. We have all the right personalities in the right jobs.

Tea holds us together. Although it may seem like a simple thing, tea sharing epitomizes the cohesion that has enabled us to keep going all these years. In lean times, team members have voluntarily taken cuts in pay to prevent layoffs. In our community, no one is "greater than." No one is above taking on any chore. We all pitch in where and when we are needed. You would never hear anyone complain, "That's not in my job description," because we do what needs to be done. We have all made sacrifices to contribute to the common good and survival of the clinic. This kind of loyalty, selflessness, and dedication is far too rare in the modern workplace.

By paying careful attention to details, relationships, and behavior, I hope to nip any potential problems in the bud. I believe the problem that you know about is not the problem that will do you in. It's the one you don't know about. This is not just my responsibility. As part of a team, I rely on my fellow members to speak up if they see something amiss. They are free to point out my errors as well. In fact, if they don't correct me when I need correcting, they get in trouble.

Our operation is small and vulnerable. It would require no effort for us to go out of business. If that happened and none of us did anything to prevent it, then we would be complicit in our own demise. To avoid that fate, we have to be a super clinic that defies the odds. Wishful thinking is not enough. We have to be extraordinary.

CREATING THE SPACE

I view team membership as the equivalent of joining Navy SEAL Team 6. We are the Special Forces of healing. We have our mission and in order to carry it out, we each have rights and responsibilities. Our responsibility is to increase the functionality of the team in every way to prevent entropy or chaos from taking over. If one of us spots a potential problem, we sound the alarm. Remaining silent is not an option. I do not expect perfection, but I do ask for total quality control. If we know of the problem, we can take action. We can even make something good come out of it.

I've seen many communities die, so I make a point of choosing near-fanatics to join the team. That's why we have a hard time finding team members. We are trying to attract exceptional people. Having the ideal person makes all the difference to our survival and success. To become part of the team, candidates have to demonstrate the ability and willingness to change. We can't afford to bring on individuals who are married to their dysfunction. They must recognize that there's always room for change. We need people who are highly functional, and there are very few of them out there. That's why the process of bringing on a new team member is so deliberate. You can tell a lot about someone if you have lunch or tea with that person consistently for two to five years. That's what we do.

Chapter 11

TOOLS FOR HEALING

"I suppose it is tempting, if the only tool you have is a hammer,
to treat everything as it if were a nail."
Abraham H. Maslow

In his 1966 book *The Psychology of Science*, psychologist Abraham Maslow describes his reaction to encountering people whose behavior did not fit comfortably with concepts and ideas he had long taken for granted. To deal with this new information, he realized, he had to either stop questioning or find new ways of answering the questions. He called this approach "problem-centering," because of its focus on the problem, as opposed to "method-centering," which applies the same method to all problems, as in the hammer analogy.

In medicine, many physicians employ medication and surgery as primary tools for healing. This narrow focus also applies to other healers, who are similarly wedded to their own modalities, whatever they may be. Having worked with Dr. Weil, I came away with the strong understanding that our loyalties must lie with our patients rather than with particular modalities. In our case conferences, we often had a dozen or more professionals representing different healing styles, such as energy healing, osteopathy, acupuncture, herbs, naturopathy, counseling, hypnosis, and shamanic work, among others.

At Georgia Integrative Medicine, we take Dr. Weil's advice to heart. We have providers who work together to listen to patients' stories. Our treatments incorporate Western medicine, Chinese medicine, energy medicine, homeopathy, and mind-body medicine. The end result is that the patients are able to benefit from a real-time integrative and a collaborative approach. It is only logical that patients receive a comprehensive assessment of their condition, including a thorough review of Western medicine. As physicians are pressured to squeeze more patients into each workday, the danger of overlooking important symptoms increases. By contrast, the integrative medicine approach can provide another level of safety for patients.

By using a full range of healing tools mindfully, we can create a convergence of healing energy for patients. For example, a disease such as osteoporosis causes brittle bones, increasing the risk of bone fracture for patients. This structural deficiency, in many cases, is the natural consequence of a biochemical disharmony affecting the structure of the bone. Poor nutrition is often a contributing factor.

Another example is heart disease. In its earlier stages, the biochemistry regulating cholesterol and inflammation modulates plaque buildup. As the disease progresses and the plaques grow, they begin to block the flow of blood to the heart. With less oxygen reaching the heart, the heart muscle deteriorates and loses its ability to pump effectively. A severe blockage can lead to a heart attack.

In both examples, it is clear that the old adage holds true. Prevention is better than a cure. But prevention requires starting interventions before the diseases have gained momentum. In many cases, simple modifications in biochemistry can lead to dramatic results in the early stages of these diseases.

The current practice of Western medicine, however, requires that there is a reason to intervene. That reason usually arrives in the form of symptoms. Unfortunately, by the time a patient notices symptoms, the disease may have progressed to a dangerous level. For example, most people who feel angina—a chest pain caused by heart muscles deprived of oxygen—have a blockage that is greater than 70 percent. At this point, many patients understandably feel that they have an urgent problem and elect to have invasive procedures such as surgery or angioplasty. In the meanwhile, it is easy for them to avoid making changes that would help prevent a further progression of their condition. By doing so, they are often simply delaying the onset of another episode of angina or a heart attack.

I prefer a comprehensive approach that takes into account a patient's mind, body, and spirit to ensure the best possible outcomes.

Pain is the symptom with which we are most familiar, both in its physical and emotional forms. Understanding the underlying causes of pain is crucial for obtaining the best results. Symptoms represent interruptions in functionality. The dysfunction can arise from structural issues, as in the cases of osteoporosis and coronary artery disease. With musculoskeletal pain, we often overlook the importance of trigger points in causing pain. Once structural issues are identified, we can make modifications in diet that will bring about positive biochemical reactions to improve health.

In addition to Western medicine, integrative medicine also has at its disposal a large toolkit of complementary and alternative therapies and techniques. Some address the physical structure of the body and others are designed to target the body's biochemistry, the chemical processes and reactions that take place within our bodies.

Tools for Healing the Structure
The most common forms of healing the structure include chiropractic, osteopathic manipulation, and massage therapy. Chiropractic involves manually manipulating the spine and other parts of the body in order to bring the body into alignment. Research shows that more

than 50 percent of Americans suffering from persistent back pain receive chiropractic treatment. Osteopathic manipulation and massage therapy similarly utilize a hands-on approach focusing on the structures and systems of the body, including bones and joints, soft tissues, and circulatory and lymphatic systems.

The tool that I find most helpful in structural healing is a form of acupuncture rarely taught in Chinese medical schools. PENS (percutaneous electrical nerve stimulation) acupuncture is also known as Craig-PENS after William Craig, the doctor who pioneered the method. I was fortunate to study briefly with Dr. Craig and continue an in-depth study with Dr. Richard Niemtzow for two years. In the PENS system, acupuncture needles are inserted close to areas of pain in conjunction with the application of an electrical current. The goal is to restore and re-educate injured muscles in a short amount of time.

The second tool that I find useful is a form of osteopathic manipulation known as Strain-Counter Strain, developed by osteopath Lawrence Jones in the 1950s. This form of manipulation seeks to alleviate pain by putting the body in natural positions of comfort for 90 seconds or more. If a muscle is in spasm, this compresses and relaxes it, allowing surrounding joints to return to normal function. As part of my fellowship at the University of Arizona, I studied with Dr. Harmon Myers, who learned the method directly from its originator, Dr. Jones. I credit Dr. Myers for giving me a thorough understanding of the musculoskeletal system of the body. Furthermore, his techniques merged well with the PENS acupuncture.

Tools to Optimize Biochemistry

Vitamins, herbs, and nutritional supplements are all examples of biochemical tools. People have used herbs to treat various ailments since ancient times. In 1991, hikers discovered the mummified remains of a man in the mountains on the Austrian-Italian border. He was thought to have lived circa 3,300 B.C. Among his personal effects was birch fungus, a medicinal plant. By the Middle Ages, thousands of botanical agents were being used for their flavor, scent, or potential therapeutic properties. Many of these, including aspirin, digitalis and quinine, form the basis of modern drugs.

At Georgia Integrative Medicine, patients often bring in bags or boxes full of supplements they have been using to self-treat their conditions. In many cases, we can reduce the number of supplements drastically and obtain an excellent result. How is this possible? Employing a systematic approach and focusing on creating synergy between supplements is the key. Seemingly unrelated symptoms can turn out to have a common cause, such as inflammation. Instead of having a multitude of supplements to treat each individual symptom, we can address the common root and see an improvement in all the symptoms.

My pharmacology training has helped me gain an appreciation for the dose-response relationship, which describes changes in the body's response depending on the level of exposure to a chemical. Overall, after having treated many people using both pharmacological agents (medications) and natural substances, I find that natural substances tend to be safer. However, it's important to be mindful of potential side effects and adverse interactions when using natural substances, especially for patients with serious illnesses. For example, with patients who are undergoing chemotherapy, a thorough understanding of the potential for medication interaction is crucial. This allows the patients to enjoy the benefits of natural supplements while avoiding possible negative interactions between chemotherapeutic agents and supplements that could result in serious consequences.

Because their widespread use dates back centuries, and because the products are "natural," many people assume dietary supplements to be inert or at least innocuous. Yet recent studies show clearly that interactions between these products and drugs do occur. For example, ginkgo biloba is the fourth most commonly used herbal supplement in the United States. It is often taken for dementia and memory enhancement, but is also prized for its antioxidant qualities. However, several reports have linked its use to an increased risk of bleeding, particularly when combined with drugs that have anticoagulant or anti-platelet effects.

Mind-Body Medicine

The patient plays a central role in mind-body medicine. Rather than remain a passive recipient, he or she is an active participant, involved in prevention, self-care, and self-healing. In this context, physicians and other providers are teachers, guides, catalysts, and sometimes conduits of healing for their patients. Mind-body medicine includes the following modalities:

- Hypnosis
- Guided imagery
- Meditation
- Yoga
- Biofeedback
- Tai Chi and Qi Gong
- Spirituality

Mind-body interventions continue to be among the most widely used forms of complementary and alternative medicine (CAM). The last National Health Interview Survey covering CAM showed that deep breathing is the most popular mind-body therapy, followed by meditation, massage, and yoga. Yoga in particular continues to grow in popularity. *Yoga Journal* reported that from 2008 to 2012, the number of Americans practicing yoga increased by an astonishing 29 percent.

In the West, the mind-body connection can be traced to the 1920s, when experimental psychologist Walter Cannon discovered a relationship between emotions and physiology. He originated the concept of the sympathetic nervous system's emergency response function, which he termed "fight or flight." Cannon described how animals' reflexes responded instinctively to perceived threats or other environmental factors.

The role of psychology in experiencing pain came into sharp focus on the battlefields of Europe, where Dr. Henry Beecher served as a military doctor during World War II. While attending the wounded at the Battle of Anzio in Italy, he noticed that despite a lack of morphine, there were injured men who seemed to feel little pain. Noting the gap between the soldiers' perceptions of pain and the reality of their injuries, he concluded that emotion had the ability to block pain. This led to his experimentation with placebos and the finding that 30 percent or more of patients who had postoperative pain received satisfactory pain relief from a placebo.

Since Beecher's time, scientists have conducted extensive research into mind-body therapies and found evidence of the benefits of certain techniques, such as biofeedback and hypnosis. Hypnosis has been shown to be successful in smoking cessation and weight loss. It can also be effective when used in conjunction with mainstream therapies—for example, to reduce the fatigue associated with chemotherapy or to support recuperation after surgery.

Tools for Healing

In recent years, mind-body medicine has highlighted the role of psychology in combating the emergence and progression of coronary artery disease. A team from UC Davis Medical Center studied a group of patients with coronary atherosclerosis who were enrolled in a two-year program of lifestyle modification that included exercise, meditation/stress reduction training, education, and counseling. The researchers concluded that such multidisciplinary programs can have a significant impact on cardiac risk factors and reduce the likelihood of subsequent cardiac events.

Mind-body methods have also proven useful in reducing pain for people suffering from conditions such as arthritis, lower back pain, and migraines and other headaches. In many cases, the benefit is greatest when treatment involves a combination of techniques. For patients suffering from potentially terminal illnesses such as cancer, mind-body therapies can have a positive overall effect in terms of improving mood and quality of life. Other benefits include the easing of treatment side effects such as nausea.

As Beecher demonstrated, our emotions can have a potent effect on blocking pain. Similarly, our emotions can affect our susceptibility to illness. We always hear about the power of positive thinking, and in fact it turns out to be true. In an article in *Psychosomatic Medicine*, Sheldon Cohen of Carnegie Mellon University and a group of colleagues reported on a study of more than

300 volunteers who were assessed for their emotional styles and then given nasal drops containing viruses for the common cold. They found that "the tendency to experience positive emotions was associated with greater resistance to developing a common cold." Other studies have linked certain psychological or emotional factors with a higher rate of respiratory infection and slower wound healing.

Energy Medicine
In my studies of healing, I have learned how energy affects our body. We use biochemical reactions to generate electricity and magnetism, which we can think of as yin and yang. The movement of electrons in the presence of a magnetic field generates electricity and the electricity generates a magnetic field.

Energy medicine uses measurable energy sources such as electromagnetic energy to modulate healing. In energy medicine, healing energy can flow from a healer to a patient. Given time, patients can be taught techniques in qi gong, tai chi, yoga, and meditation that utilize their own biofield energy for self-healing.

The use of energy in healing, even in conventional medicine, is well established. Consider cardiac pacemakers, which make use of electrical signals to keep the heart beating regularly. An MRI (magnetic resonance imaging) test uses a magnetic field and radio waves to capture internal images of the body.

Magnets produce a magnetic field that is thought by some to be helpful in pain relief. As a result, there are a number of products containing magnets available on the market today. They are especially popular with those suffering from conditions such as fibromyalgia, arthritis, and sports-related injuries. Current scientific knowledge does not confirm the painkilling effect of these static magnets

The aforementioned PENS acupuncture uses electrical current in specific frequencies to stimulate nerves, nerve roots and the nervous system in order to reduce pain. This is an example of how an input of energy can bring about positive changes in structure. In PENS acupuncture, determining the correct frequency and the placement of needles are paramount to success. Most muscle conditions will respond to a frequency of about 1 to 2 hertz, which corresponds to the beating of our heart, which is composed of muscles.

Have you ever closed your eyes and relaxed to the sounds of a mellow CD? If so, you have benefited from sound therapy. There is a reason massage therapists put on soothing instrumental music while performing massages. Music therapy has been associated with a reduction in blood pressure, heart rate, and stress. Generally speaking, it makes us feel better, calmer, more at peace. Sound therapy encompasses both recorded and live music and the creation of healing sounds through the use of instruments such as tuning forks, bowls, and gongs. Sometimes imagery is employed as an accompaniment.

Light therapy involves the use of natural or artificial light. People suffering from seasonal affective disorder, a form of depression related to the passing of summer and the onset of winter, have found that exposure to a light box mimicking sunlight relieves their symptoms. Psoriasis is a chronic autoimmune disease that presents on the skin. Ultraviolet light B (UVB) treatments are considered an effective treatment for psoriasis and can be achieved either through exposure to natural sunlight or with the use of an UVB light unit.

Laser therapy is most associated with its use in eye surgery, but it is also used in procedures such as kidney stone removal, prostate removal, the treatment of varicose veins, and to remove moles and other marks from the skin.

I have already talked about qi, the Chinese term for the vital energy of the universe that flows through everything, and about the importance of maintaining harmony and balance. In the Chinese tradition, all forms of a person's health—physical, mental, emotional—are linked to these concepts. Consequently, Chinese medicine focuses on restoring balance and enabling the natural flow of qi. The idea of energy is central. In acupuncture, needles are placed along the meridians that conduct qi through the body, thus removing any blockages and allowing energy to flow freely once again. Qi gong, like tai chi, is a form of physical movement that incorporates mental focus and deep breathing while seeking to optimize the flow of qi.

Reiki, in which practitioners place their hands either on or close to a patient's body with the intent of generating healing energy, is another well-known mind-body practice. Although there is no solid scientific evidence proving its health benefits, it is considered generally safe when used together with conventional medicine.

At Georgia Integrative Medicine, we use a variety of energy healing devices utilizing light frequencies, sound frequencies, electric currents, and magnetic fields. These devices help us to understand our patients' conditions and provide a wide array of tools to explore what might be helpful to our patients. In addition, team members are strongly encouraged to learn energy healing modalities such as reiki or tai chi. This allows them to have firsthand knowledge of the healing modalities used in the clinic.

In trying to understand a patient's condition, we draw from four different medical philosophies: homeopathy, Chinese medicine, naturopathy, and integrative medicine.

Homeopathy

Homeopathy is a therapeutic system that uses natural remedies to produce in patients symptoms that are similar to the symptoms of their diseases, in the belief that "like cures like." The founder of homeopathy, 18th century German physician Samuel Hahnemann observed that quinine, used to treat malaria, caused malarial symptoms in healthy individuals, and deduced that substances that caused symptoms similar to a specific disease could also cure that disease. He also believed the smaller the dose, the greater the efficacy. The result is that homeopathic remedies are often highly diluted, to the point where they contain little trace of the original substance.

Chinese Medicine

Chinese medicine is an ancient system of healing that encompasses a variety of different treatments, all based on the notion of yin and yang, the two opposing yet complementary forces of the universe; and on the concept of *qi*. Unlike in Western medicine, treatments in Chinese medicine are tailored specifically to the needs of the individual patient after a thorough analysis. This means that patients exhibiting similar symptoms may be receiving completely different treatments. Herbal medicine and acupuncture are the best known forms of Chinese medicine in the West.

Naturopathy

Naturopathy emphasizes the healing power of nature and values the body's ability to heal itself. Naturopathic treatments include the use of homeopathy, herbal medicine, nutrition and lifestyle counseling, and massage therapy. The following principles form the basis of naturopathic practice:

- First do no harm.
- Enable the healing power of nature.
- Treat the causes of disease, not the symptoms.
- Educate patients.
- Treat the whole person
- Work to prevent illness.

Integrative Medicine
Integrative medicine encompasses all healing possibilities but owes allegiance to none. Practitioners of different traditions such as acupuncturists, chiropractors, naturopaths, homeopaths, and Western physicians often exhibit a bias towards their system of healing. As Maslow's observation reminds us, blind loyalty to one modality leaves us unable to view the situation clearly. Not every problem is a nail. The patient always comes first. What can we do to alleviate his or her suffering?

At Georgia Integrative Medicine, we offer expertise in many healing modalities, but above all, we offer a commitment to patient healing, however that may be achieved.

CHAPTER 12

GOOD BUSINESS

In business, be competent.
Tao Te Ching

Over the years, I have had the opportunity to witness firsthand several business enterprises. I remember my meeting with the business manager of one venture, based in an academic setting. Looking at the financial statement, I commented, "You are going out of business in six months." Though she may have been perplexed by my statement, the program did indeed close within six months. In another program, I served on a committee charged with reviewing financial information. I told them that they would be forced to close the program within the next several years unless fundamental equations were changed. They considered my input pessimistic and outlandish, and I was excused from further meetings. Three years later, I received an announcement saying that the program was ending due to unaffordable operating costs.

From the beginning, it was clear to me that in order to ensure success and longevity, we would need to implement sound business practices. Good intentions alone do not pay the bills or keep the doors open. I also wanted to show that smart business principles and a compassionate workplace are not mutually exclusive, as many corporations have led us to believe. In other words, we don't have to sacrifice our humanity to make money, but we do sometimes have to sacrifice. As Jeanne mentioned, we have operated with a flexible payroll when our accounts were down. At the beginning, we worked long hours for minimal pay, confident in the knowledge that the effort we were putting in would be returned to us manifold when the business was up and running. At times, it was precarious, but we survived.

After seven years, we have a different set of problems. We are beginning to have capacity issues. Our patients now have to wait up to two weeks to see a provider. Time and space issues present a big challenge. We would also like to add new team members, but finding the right person organically has proven to be a tall order, especially given the length and investment of time required to evaluate an individual's suitability.

Our business model differs from that of other medical organizations. We do not deal with insurance companies. Instead, we offer an a la carte menu of services, along with yearly memberships. Patient members pay an annual fee, as well as a co-pay of $30 to $60 per visit. This model is relatively recent for us. When we first started out, we didn't have the reputation and track record to implement a membership system. It took time for patients to find the clinic, become acquainted with us, and ultimately, trust us with their health and wellness. Now that we have established ourselves in the community, many new patients come to us through referrals. The trust and reputation have been built up enough so that people are willing to make the investment. Those who have been with us for years like the memberships. For us, it is also a way to gauge the commitment level of prospective patients. If people aren't serious about improving their health from the outset, they are the ones who are more likely to drop off over time. We are looking for patients who will commit to this practice, and many have. While we currently still offer non-membership service options, it is likely that we will move to a membership-only model in the near future.

In return for membership, patients receive year-round access to a team of healers. This form of concierge medicine is growing in popularity across medical fields, but is especially suited to integrative medicine, which already places a high value on personalized treatment. In keeping with the integrative approach, we treat patients as a team rather than in a disjointed, perfunctory fashion. This means that our collective efforts and talents go into the treating of each patient. This is very different from other medical practices. In many conventional clinics, you are lucky to see one medical doctor, much less a whole team. As doctors are expected to take on more and more patients, accessibility becomes an issue. An increase in volume leads to an increase in overcapacity, effectively creating a choke point that prevents people from easily accessing health care.

In an insurance-based system, people have no idea how much money they're actually paying for their health care. They may know what their premium is, but trying to decipher an explanation of benefits statement can be like trying to unlock a secret code. The numbers appear random. Most of the money is exchanged between the insurance company and the provider, so we never see it. Physicians are not paid to solve problems or to keep us well; they are paid to complete procedures and move patients along to the next stage in the medical factory: specialist, hospital, pharmacy, laboratory. In our model, people know what they are paying for up front; there are no hidden or inflated charges and no surprises.

To succeed, integrative medicine must be more than a collection of modalities gathered in one place. It must be implemented as a whole. In practice, it must espouse wellness for employees as well as for patients. In my visits to other integrative medicine facilities, I often noticed the absence of teambuilding. Many practitioners operated in fear under the tyranny of administrators who were themselves scrutinized by hospital executives. Even in integrative medicine, with its supposed focus on mindfulness and mind-body medicine, bureaucracy was ever present.

I believe that integrative medicine without integrity cannot fulfill its potential. Similarly, integrative medicine organizations that operate out of fear will never rise to the occasion. From my observations, the failed integrative medicine clinics had one characteristic in common. They all lacked integrity. The formula is simple. Practice compassion, moderation, and humility to serve your patients. Be patient. Be yourself. Relax. Surround yourself with an outstanding team. Invest in the loss. Stick to the principles, even when it hurts your margins in short run. Survive to serve another day.

At the end of the day, an integrative medicine clinic is still a business. All the clinics I worked in operated using the latest business processes such as total quality control, just in time inventory, and an inventory-stocking system based on probability. Technology and automation have simplified many routine functions and made it possible to do more with fewer resources. However, there are some aspects of business for which there are no shortcuts. One is leadership.

Servant leadership allows room for empowering employees to fulfill their passion, which in turn inspires people to perform beyond expected norms, with increased productivity, and loyalty. The most expensive portion of a business operation is often the payroll. Yet most companies do not invest enough in their employees. Simple employee satisfaction is not enough. If a company does not provide for the wellness of employees, they will leave as soon as they are offered a better deal elsewhere. Employee loyalty grows only when the organization is willing to invest substantially in employees.

These are the beliefs that guide us as we continue to build Georgia Integrative Medicine. We intend to be an integral organization, exemplifying how a company can offer excellence to clients while serving its employees. We firmly believe that how we treat employees translates into how employees respond to our clients. These are not revolutionary ideas—take a look at successful companies like Starbucks and Google.

Many of the medical organizations I visited rely heavily on part-time workers and independent contractors. This has an obvious financial benefit for the company. Part-time employees do not receive benefit packages. Independent contractors pay their own taxes. However, this creates an environment of insecurity for part-time workers, who do not enjoy the stability of a full-time, permanent position. Instead of creating a collegial atmosphere, it leads to an atmosphere of competitiveness, where people are pitted against one another.

In my experience, a reliance on part-time employment provides a façade of togetherness for the patients, but prevents true bonding between co-workers. Rather than conveying a sense of "we're all in it together," it reinforces individual isolation and a "survival of the fittest" mentality. At Georgia

Integrative Medicine, I was determined to avoid this situation. Everyone at our clinic is an employee, not an independent consultant, and preferably an employee with full-time status. We are in the process of defining full time as three full days a week so that team members can retain time for their families, especially if they have young children.

This distinction has a far-reaching impact on work life. As an employee, you're paid regardless of whether or not you see patients. You're not dependent on meeting a quota of visits to get paid. Your salary is guaranteed. If the clinic does well, everyone receives a bonus. This setup creates a different dynamic. We are not pitting people against one another. There is no way to do well individually. We rise or fall together, so naturally we strive to rise.

Author Stephen Covey, in his book *The 8th Habit: From Effectiveness to Greatness*, wrote, "Despite all our gains in technology, product innovation and world markets, most people are not thriving in the organizations they work for." By this, he means that people feel disengaged from their work, unsure of their organizational mission, and generally frustrated in their professional lives. Given the amount of time people spend at their jobs, this is a sad comment on modern society. Increasingly, individuals are seeking out alternatives to the traditional 9 to 5 office job that offer more meaning, autonomy, and fulfillment.

Good Business

To empower our employees, we take account of everyone's input before undertaking major decisions. We offer supplementary benefits. Georgia Integrative Medicine currently offers organic meals to employees, provides nutritional supplements while at work, and pays for educational expenses. Jeanne will tell you that she is covered from the tip of her toes to the top of her head, which is to say that everything from her hair coloring to her special orthopedic shoe inserts are paid for by the company.

There is no question that our greatest assets are our people. By taking good care of them and ensuring that their needs are met, we create a continuous wave of positive energy that continues on to our patients and back again, feeding and nourishing us. This cycle of giving and receiving sustains us. This means providing the best ergonomic chairs, the most advanced and reliable computers, and state-of-the-art equipment. We could make do with adequate equipment, but we are not aiming to be adequate. We want to be exceptional. Part of this is anticipating and preventing negative consequences. Maybe someone doesn't have a bad back now, but sitting for an extended period of time in a cheap office chair could potentially cause back problems. That is something I want to prevent.

Healers are notorious for not taking good care of themselves because they are too busy taking care of their patients. I don't want anyone at Georgia

Integrative Medicine to fall into bad habits and jeopardize their own health. This has been a difficult lesson for some. I remind Jeanne that if she over-schedules team members today, we will not have them tomorrow.

Of course you want to take good care of your patients, but you can't do that if your providers are worn out. We are not interested in using people up and spitting them out. We want to keep them around for the long haul, so I emphasize the importance of self-care. We are the instruments of healing that keep our company going. If we are ailing, we cannot be of service to our patients. Consequently, team members have access to regular treatments of their own choosing to maintain and sustain their individual wellness.

Employees who feel supported and cared for do better work and look for ways to support and advance the company. I need team members to show initiative and be proactive rather than reactive. This requires people who care, who have the desire to improve their workplace. I believe that the success or failure of a corporation is found in its soul. Many employers pay lip service to ethical behavior and claim to offer ideal working conditions, but when you scratch the surface of these claims, you will often find they are nothing more than empty words. In our hyper capitalist society, we have placed a premium on profit, speed, growth, and coming in first. The notion of operating any other way is perceived as strange, possibly weak, and certainly not good business.

In the teachings of Buddhism, the Eightfold Path is a guide to living which, if practiced correctly, can lead to enlightenment and a release from suffering. However, you don't need to be a Buddhist to benefit from the clear blueprint the Eightfold Path offers for a life lived well. The eight components of the path are: right understanding, right intention, right speech, right action, right livelihood, right effort, right mindfulness, and right concentration. They fall into three categories: wisdom, ethical conduct, and mental discipline. How many modern CEOs would measure up well against these standards?

Take the case of J.C. Penney, one of the nation's most well known retail chains. When Ron Johnson was recruited from Apple to try and turn around the struggling company in 2011, he received a signing bonus of $52.7 million in shares. Johnson lost his job 17 months later, but not before laying off 19,000 employees and plunging the company even deeper into trouble. Still, *Forbes* magazine had the audacity to congratulate him for accepting a "tiny" exit package of just under $150,000. This was in addition to his $1.5 million base salary.

Unfortunately, this is not a rare exception in the corporate world, where leaders are so far removed from workers that they seem to breathe a different air, and where the bottom line really is the bottom line. At Georgia Integrative Medicine, we seek to adhere to tenets that would sound familiar to Buddhists. We have only a few established rules. The first is to practice good judgment at all times. The second rule is to act with compassion, moderation, and humility. A third rule is to lead by serving and lead by example. Following these rules requires strength of character and self-awareness.

Of course we do not expect people to accomplish all this on their own. After all, we are a team. We are here to support each other. I firmly believe that our investments in our employees will pay dividends with a superior healing experience for patients. I have already spoken of the merits of tea sharing, but we also share meals when possible. Nutrition plays a central role in our healing treatments, and also in our own wellness. The company provides meals three times a week and we often go out to eat as a group. In the clinic's early days, Nola would cook every day. Now that we are busier, she cooks less frequently, but we are still lucky enough to enjoy her food on a regular basis. For a typical lunch, she might offer a meal of lima beans prepared in a slow cooker with onions, leeks, celery, smoked sun-dried tomatoes, fresh ground mustard seed and other spices, served with sweet potatoes, okra, and cornbread made from rice flour, amaranth, and flaxseeds.

Like tea sharing, communal eating accelerates social bonding. We often celebrate birthdays by having potlucks. In addition, I try to share a meal with a team member outside the clinic once a month. Activities outside of work offer opportunities to build emotional deposits, creating a deeper social context. In addition, we travel to conferences together if we can. Nothing helps to build a team like traveling to a new place, eating, playing, and building memories together.

The result of all these collaborative activities is a tight emotional bonding based on love and deep friendship. Many patients tell us that they feel a sense of peaceful harmony and love when they walk in the clinic. This emanates from a group of people who have shared meaningful experiences over a period of years, who have persisted through conditions that were not always easy, and come to know and care for one another in a multi-dimensional way, not just as co-workers. We are able to trust one another and know that we have each other's best interests at heart because they are inseparable from our own best interests.

We subscribe to the egalitarian principles that flow from servant leadership. From the round tea table to the group input on choosing new team members to shared duties, we take this concept seriously. Taking care of our environment includes doing housework, and no one is exempt. We use real sheets; therefore, linens must be washed each and every day. We split the laundry up equally. Although I could exclude myself from this task, I don't. That way, the burden of laundry is divided equally among us. I also prepare rooms, empty trash, cook, and clean, just like everyone else. I do not let myself fall into the trap of thinking that I am in any way better or more deserving than anyone or that my time is more valuable.

Hierarchical structures dominate in the corporate world, as well as in medicine. In a medical setting, where lives are at stake, this built-in hierarchy can have dangerous consequences. Senior physicians are not used to having their opinions and decisions questioned. In the cinematic thriller *Malice*, Alec Baldwin plays a surgeon who is sued for damages by a patient. During a deposition, his character is asked if he has a God complex. His response is a scathing, narcissistic monologue that ends chillingly, "You ask me if I have a God complex. Let me tell you something: I am God."

While not every surgeon possesses this level of hubris, it is true that the traditional superior-subordinate setup stifles innovation and encourages intimidation. Those in the upper echelons do not like to be second-guessed; those in the lower ranks are fearful of voicing concerns when they witness an oversight or come to a different conclusion than their bosses. The losers are the patients.

At Georgia Integrative Medicine, what we aim for is the complete opposite. We call each other team members because people don't work *for* me; they work *with* me.

If I wanted to find people to rubber stamp everything I say in return for a paycheck, it would be easy. What is difficult is finding people whose standards are so high that they could not let anything pass that does not meet those standards, people who form careful, considered opinions and do not hesitate to share them.

Being assertive does not come naturally to everyone. Jeanne is not afraid to let me know what she thinks, even if she believes I won't like what she has to say. She adheres to the concept of telling the truth without fear of consequences. This can lead to conflict when we disagree, and sometimes we have to call in Vena to render a final decision. But I want to hear that contrarian position because I am not wedded to my own infallibility. If there's a better way of doing things, I want to know about it.

Because there is always room for growth, continual improvement is an ongoing process. In her story, Dorothy referred to my method as "poking." For example, I may ask questions simply to evaluate someone's responses, which give me an insight into what and how they're thinking. In the same vein, I may challenge someone to move beyond her comfort zone in order to grow. This goes back to the tai chi technique of pushing hands, in which two people maintain light contact with one another and attempt to maintain balance. Just as we can easily become attached to our dysfunctional relationships, we become comfortable with our individual neuroses. The ability to transform and change is key to fulfilling our true potential as human beings. When we look for new team members, we are looking for a person who is willing to change and who can take constructive correction. As for myself, I too am on a continual quest for self-improvement and I rely on the team to challenge me as I challenge them.

This type of workplace is not for everyone. It requires a certain level of dedication above and beyond what is expected of a typical employee. We seek people with not only a commitment to integrative medicine, but to an integral organization.

CHAPTER 13

A DAY IN THE LIFE

Only when we are sick of our sickness shall we cease to be sick.
Tao te Ching

In the early 1960s, a small town in eastern Pennsylvania came to the attention of two researchers. Roseto, founded by Italian immigrants, is a town of fewer than 2,000 residents located in the foothills of the Appalachian Mountains. Stewart Wolf, a medical doctor, and sociologist John G. Bruhn became interested in Roseto when they discovered that the male death rate from heart attack was less than half that of neighboring towns. Intrigued, the researchers set out to discover why.

At first, it was thought that perhaps their Mediterranean diet played a role. Did they exercise more? Smoke less? Inherit great genes? Residents underwent physical exams. They completed family surveys. Dietitians observed their food shopping and eating habits. Surprisingly, the results showed that people in Roseto ate the same animal fats as other Americans, smoked as much, exercised as little, and suffered from hypertension and diabetes at the same rate as their counterparts in the region. The researchers were stumped, until they began to notice that the town possessed certain characteristics that were not in evidence elsewhere. The population was very homogenous and tightly knit. Most families lived in multi-generational households. People supported and looked out for one another with a sense of community and solidarity. Their sense of identity and cohesion was reinforced by shared religion, culture, history, and traditions.

As Wolf and Bruhn noted in their retrospective, *The Power of Clan*, "What seems to have been learned is an old but often forgotten conviction that mutual respect and cooperation contribute to the health and welfare of a community and its inhabitants, and that self-indulgence and lack of concern for others exert opposite influences."

Over time, as the town grew more heterogeneous, younger residents became more integrated into the world outside Roseto and began to move away from the ways of their parents and grandparents, living independently and abandoning old-world traditions. Deaths by heart attack started to climb correspondingly until they reached the same levels as in surrounding towns. The "Roseto effect" disappeared

As Americans, we value diversity, so we are not looking to replicate a physical Roseto, with its notable homogeneity. Americans also move around more than any other people in the world, so our neighborhoods are often in flux. How then, do we create the kind of community the people of Roseto enjoyed for generations? That is what we are attempting at Georgia Integrative Medicine. We want to create an atmosphere that provides the kind of support, encouragement, and nurturing that can have a Roseto-like effect on people's physical and emotional well-being. We want this for our patients as well as for ourselves.

As I mentioned, people walking into the clinic tell us they feel a difference as soon as they come through our door. But the process starts even before that. Our first contact is usually over the phone. Prospective patients call in to find our more about our services and if we can help them. During that initial call, we find out more about a patient's condition and what they are hoping for from us. Almost all the patients who come to us have already visited other health care providers. Consider Dorothy's case. She had exhausted the conventional medical options and was at the end of her rope. Dorothy is representative of many of our patients. The medical establishment has often given up on them and they are closing to giving up themselves.

On the phone, we try to assess our ability to help someone. We are not in business to give people false hope. We do not take on cancer patients who can no longer eat or who are dependent on oxygen. There are plenty of practitioners who will lie to patients to get their business. We are committed to truth. We do have patients with cancer, but we are very clear with them about what we can and cannot do. Our focus in these cases is to help optimize patients' healing potential and improve their quality of life through nutrition. We also work to improve immune function, support energy levels, and help individuals cope with the side effects of traditional cancer treatments. Other patients might have issues ranging from lupus to infertility to autoimmune diseases. Some come for primary care services. Many suffer from chronic pain.

During the important first contact, we answer people's questions and give them information on our fees. The next step is an integrative needs assessment, which typically lasts 20 to 30 minutes. During this session, I meet with the patient to discuss his or her health care concerns and goals and to evaluate how I can be of service. The assessment does not include treatment.

Next comes the initial integrative medicine visit. During the visit, I review medical history, available labs or medical records, and take note of any medications, vitamins, supplements, or herbs the patient is currently taking. The visit can take a full two hours because really getting to know someone takes time. Some doctors work with a "treat and street" attitude, meaning that they offer some quick treatment solution – often a referral, prescription, or test – and then send the patient away. I heard the case of one woman who went to a doctor for what she feared might be a broken finger. After looking at an x-ray, the doctor told the woman that the finger was not broken. When the patient had questions, the doctor sighed and said, "I wish I had a DVD player in here so I could just play it instead of repeating the same thing to different patients." She made no attempt to hide the fact that for her, talking to patients had become tedious.

If you are used to cursory, impersonal interactions with doctors, the integrative medical experience will feel very different. It will be much more reassuring and validating. When I visit with patients, I am trying to understand why the patient is there. I want to get a sense of the big picture, learn what has already been done and hear what other physicians have recommended. The examination incorporates Western medicine, naturopathic medicine, and Chinese medicine. I use my findings to formulate an individualized treatment plan for each patient. All appropriate therapies, both conventional and alternative, are considered. Although we do not prescribe narcotics, I will prescribe mainstream pharmaceuticals when necessary. If I think someone needs antibiotics, I will prescribe them. Depending on the plan devised, treatment may incorporate one or more of the following:

- Chinese medicine
- Craniosacral therapy
- Energy medicine

- Food as Medicine (Nutrition)
- Homeopathy
- Mind/body medicine
- Naturopathy
- Western Medicine

In taking on a new patient, I am entering into a therapeutic relationship. It is a two-way street, and I expect the patient to participate fully in the healing process. I commit to it as a long-term relationship. In order for the partnership to work, we need to keep all the options open. It won't work, for example, if a patient comes in asking for a particular type of treatment and rejecting all others. For our part, we provide a team effort. Cases are shared among the team, giving patients the benefit of multiple perspectives and integrated care.

The modalities we offer do not differ greatly from other integrative medicine facilities, although we are the only clinic I know of to have a full-time, in-house provider offering classical homeopathy. Many integrative medicine facilities will erect a building and assemble people with varying skill sets and backgrounds to perform therapies, but they put no thought into creating a team. The result is akin to a network of railroad tracks going off in opposite directions. In order to keep from derailing, patients have to continuously switch tracks. Our approach, on the other hand, is seamless because we are always working in tandem to ensure coordinated treatment for each patient.

A Day in the Life

We see approximately 15 to 18 patients a day. The clinic has three treatment rooms and a consultation room, so we can have up to four at one time, but as I said, we are careful not to overschedule. We also make a point of not filling the daily schedule ahead of time in case there are last minute patient appointments. We always leave room for contingencies because we anticipate some-one may call and need help immediately. This is in stark contrast to many medical practices, which overbook their schedules, leading to crowded waiting rooms and long delays.

Every morning we come in. Jeanne prints the calendar and begins assigning rooms for the patients who will come in that day. She, Nola, and I will have a cup of tea and start seeing patients. Nola serves as my medical assistant and is the first point of contact for patients af-ter they check in. Her job is not only to screen patients for physical symptoms, but also to serve a counseling function by listening and evaluating their psychological condition. That way she can pass on to me any informa-tion about their state of mind that might be affecting their health and wellness.

The reason why we take so much time with each patient and personalize treatments is because we know that human beings are complex. Western medicine is based on a paradigm of repeatability and predictability. If you go to your car and start the engine, it starts. If it doesn't start, you take it to a mechanic, who replaces a part.

Then you put the key in and it starts again. The problem is that the world we live in is not so simple. Our lives are very unpredictable. While we may have routines, we never live the same day twice. When you factor in the complexity of human beings, the paradigm fails. Health too is complex, shaped by a multitude of factors, including genetics, lifestyle, social support, emotional and mental states, geography, and more.

At Georgia Integrative Medicine, we are healers. Healing restores people to wholeness. This is distinct from curing, which focuses on recovery from disease. Realistically, we know that life carries a 100 percent mortality rate, but we struggle against that truth. We expect medicine to fight death, but it cannot possibly succeed. Instead of focusing on a cure, we need to focus on healing. If we accept that life is impermanent and mortality is inevitable, we can accept healing. A cure may be impossible, but there is plenty of healing that can take place throughout our lives.

Because we focus on healing and not curing, we are available to you all the time, not just when you are sick or hurting. When it comes to our health, it is our tendency to react to situations as they arise. We wait until we're not feeling well and then decide to take action. Even then, seeing a doctor is a last resort for many people. We treat our cars with more care. Do you take your car in for an oil change regularly? We have been programmed to understand that we need to take our cars in for service even when they're running smoothly, in order to prevent bigger problems down the road. Cars are replaceable; people are not. If you're not making your own wellness at least as much of a priority as your vehicle, then you are also likely to have bigger problems awaiting you down the road.

We seek to help you with healing in all its dimensions— physical, emotional, mental, social, and spiritual. This is not something that is done to you, but a process in which you are fully engaged. No one can unilaterally restore you to wholeness; you must be involved. We have patients who say that they have given up hope by the time they reach us, but the truth is that if they had truly given up hope, they wouldn't be at our door. This means that they still possess the capacity to heal, if they choose to do so. And because we are not wedded to cures, this healing possibility applies to all our patients, even those who are in the later stages of cancer.

The Tao emphasizes effectiveness and efficiency, putting in the minimum effort that will give you the maximum results. The mainstream medical community is very efficient in seeing patients. Patients travel in and out of doctors' offices in a continuous procession. However, it is clear that they are not effective. If we have such a great health care system and are so technologically and scientifically advanced, why is it that we still face such high rates of diabetes, heart disease, and obesity?

Because many of our patients have already been to see other medical professionals at highly respected health organizations and received no relief, you might imagine that their cases are not the easiest to manage. Of course there are cases where I am not able to help or find the answers they are looking for. However, I'm glad to say that in 80 to 90 percent of cases, we are able to achieve very satisfactory results as measured by patient satisfaction. Part of the process on our end is continual evaluation of a patient's progress.

Looking back at the Pennsylvania town of Roseto, we see another characteristic of its residents was resilience in the face of hardship. As newcomers to this country, they faced prejudice and harsh treatment at the hands of the English and Welsh immigrants who lived in adjacent communities. Overwhelming discrimination from the external population reinforced the Italians' reliance on one another and bonded them together even more closely. To be isolated is hard enough in good times, but when times get rough, it is unbearable. Not everyone has familial ties or a social network to support them. Part of Nola's daily routine is to call patients and check on them. We consider our patients part of our community. We are interested in their welfare not only when they're in our treatment room, but throughout their lives. What happens in the clinic is inseparable from what happens to them at home. It is all interconnected.

Nola mentioned an elderly patient who found it cathartic to simply talk. This speaks to the deep human need to connect and to be heard. Imagine holding on to feelings of bitterness for an entire lifetime and how it might feel to finally let those toxins leave your system. Diseases can be infectious, but so can feelings. Most of us have been in a situation where someone came into a room and the mood immediately took a nosedive, or have known a person who was so relentlessly negative that he or she became known as a "downer." This also holds true for positive feelings. If a yawn is contagious, then so too is a smile.

It may sound strange to describe a clinic as a loving place, but if you visit us, you will begin to understand why it fits. We care for each other and for our patients with loving compassion. This goes beyond the treatment we offer. Jeanne crochets blankets to give to patients for one reason or another, but mostly for love of that person. Dorothy and Nola have joined together to play beautiful music for patients. We are able to go this extra mile for our patients because we are always focused on our mission. We remain self-aware and mindful and we look after ourselves so we will be able to continue providing excellent services. The proof, as they say, is in the pudding. We have patients who travel long distances to reach us, including a patient who drives in from another state. We have a steady pool of volunteers because patients enjoy being with us and like spending time in the clinic. They will come in to help out or occasionally cook for us. Word-of-mouth is our biggest marketing tool, which tells us that people like what we are doing.

When we struck out on this adventure in 2007, there was no way to predict where we would be today. Now, when we project five or 10 years into the future, we still cannot say for certain where we will be. What we do know is that we will continue to follow the path where it leads, staying true to our principles. The clinic will grow at its own pace as more people realize the value of integrative health and tire of cookie cutter medicine. Jeanne uses the metaphor of an ark to describe the clinic. As she sees it, we have rowed through many storms together. This activity has made us strong and fit and we will continue rowing, never content simply to float.

EPILOGUE

A recent editorial in *The New York Times* titled "The Shame of American Health Care" reiterated yet again the monumental hurdles we face in the health care arena. Compared with other industrial nations, all of which have universal or near-universal health care, we pay far more for far less. According to the piece, more than a third of Americans go without recommended care, do not see a doctor when they are sick, or fail to fill prescriptions because of cost.

The cost of health care is untenable. Every year, health care expenditures outpace other economic expenditures, burdening individuals, businesses, and our government. At the same time, the population is aging, leading to higher social security costs, greater health care outlays, and decreased tax revenue. Economists are deeply concerned about the potential crises resulting from a combination of natural resource shortages, ecological changes, demographic shifts, a growing trade imbalance, and federal deficits.

Crisis can be a powerful catalyst for change. In the early 20th century, our society overcame a public health crisis involving infectious illnesses by adopting a comprehensive approach that included the application of new technologies such as microbiology, biochemistry, and pharmacology. Most importantly, officials instituted extensive public health measures. I believe that a similar broad approach is needed to address the epidemic of chronic illnesses rampant in our modern society.

With an increase in life expectancy, people often live for decades with chronic conditions such as hypertension, diabetes, and coronary artery diseases. Unlike infectious diseases, chronic illnesses often involve a complex interaction of genetics, biology, and behavior. It is likely that an effective strategy will require a multidisciplinary effort incorporating input from the fields of medicine, psychology, sociology, and public health. In other words, a holistic and integrative approach to health care will be necessary.

Unfortunately, the current focus in health care policy appears to be limited to boosting access to insurance. It is true that we need better access to affordable, efficient, and compassionate health care. However, the problem is not limited to affordability and efficiency. It is also about effectiveness. Is it possible that our technologically oriented medicine does not work as well for complex medical problems involving behavioral issues, such as obesity? And if technological innovation is the solution to our problems, why is it that addiction continues to be a problem for many people? Efforts to "fix" the health care system do not examine or address intrinsic failures in the current system. Consequently, even if access is expanded, it will simply offer greater access to a failed system.

There is a story of a man searching for a key under a street lamp. A passerby stops to help with the search. They are not able to find the key. When the passerby asks the man where he dropped the key, he points to a spot in the dark and says, "I lost it over there." Why, then, is he looking under the street lamp? "Because," he replies, "that's where the light is." Unfortunately, it seems we are intent on trying to solve our current problems with tools that are familiar but ineffective.

The failure of our medical systems to adequately deal with complex chronic illnesses is evident in many ways. The cost of medical care will keep rising as we continue to practice a reactive form of medicine that waits for symptoms to appear, triggering a medical emergency. Once a situation becomes urgent, there are established protocols to treat the illness. Often, the treatments do not include a comprehensive prevention strategy, so patients lurch from crisis to crisis.

We all have an opportunity to contribute either to the problem or to the solution. It begins with awareness. The second step is to understand the complexity of the issue and begin taking small steps without being attached to any particular outcome. We must understand that our intent, belief, and behavior toward healing can have a genuine influence on the practice of medicine.

Public and private organizations and corporations will have to increase investment in infrastructures promoting wellness. Creating sustainable social and economic incentives is crucial. The force needed to create this revolution is not likely to come from corporations or government. As individuals, we must become proponents of change.

When I first started the integrative health care movement in Georgia, it was as one person wanting to create a successful, sustainable, and equitable integrative medicine company. Now, we have a team working together to grow a community of healers. I believe that everyone has a unique destiny. No matter what our circumstances are, we have choices to make that will determine the path our lives take.

More information on the clinic and our team is available on our website at www.georgiaintegrativemedicine. com. If you are interested in making a positive change by learning more about our work or joining our community as a patient or team member, we look forward to hearing from you.

Yoon Hang "John" Kim, MD

NOTES/SOURCES

There are numerous English translations of the *Tao Te Ching*. The versions I consulted for this book are *Tao Te Ching*, by Stephen Mitchell (Harper & Row, 1988) and *A New Way of Thinking, A New Way of Being: Experiencing the Tao Te Ching*, by Dr. Wayne W. Dyer (Hay House, 2010).

I also drew on the following books for quotes and insights.

The 8th Habit: From Effectiveness to Greatness by Stephen R. Covey (Free Press, 2004)

Principle-Centered Leadership by Stephen R. Covey (Fireside Press, 1992)

The Psychology of Science: A Reconnaissance by Abraham H. Maslow (Joanna Cotler Books, 1966)

The Psychopath Test: A Journey Through the Madness Industry by Jon Ronson (Riverhead Books, 2011)

The Power of Clan: The Influence of Human Relationships on Heart Disease by Stewart Wolf and John G. Bruhn (Transaction Publishers, 1998)

For those interested in the PBS series *Healing and the Mind*, the full DVD set is available for purchase from the PBS store (www.shoppbs.org). There is also a book to accompany the series: *Healing and the Mind* by Bill Moyers (Doubleday, 1993).